COMPETENT CREW

Practical Course Notes

This booklet is aimed at illustrating and clarifying the practical courses run by the RYA. Lack of space has forced us to condense these notes to the bare essentials and leave you to find out about the most enjoyable part – THE SAILING!

TO BEGIN WITH ...

If you've never lived on a boat before it might all seem rather cramped at first but you'll soon appreciate that space isn't everything when afloat.

As you'll all be living at quite close-quarters be sure to tell the skipper if you are taking any form of medicine, so he'll know what action to take if anything goes wrong.

Sea sickness sufferers will probably feel better on a small sailing yacht than they would on a large rolling ship. However take along your favourite remedy as any vomiting can upset the effectiveness of medication, including the contraceptive pill!

Rules on alcohol and tobacco vary from boat to boat, *BUT any form of illegal drug found aboard could lead to the confiscation of the vessel.*

RYA recognised sea schools provide all safety equipment and often lend or hire out waterproofs and seaboots.
(*See page 25 for details, if you decide to buy your own.*)

Weather afloat can vary from hot to *very* cold and wet, so your choice of clothes should reflect this. But, as space is limited (and sometimes damp) pack everything in plastic bags and then into a *soft* holdall or kitbag.

Shirts and trousers should not leave a chilling gap when you bend over and all footwear should have 'non-slip' soles. Glasses, sun hats and knives need to be tied on and a woolly hat will keep your head warm at night. Special sailing gloves can be bought if your hands need protection and rings ought to be left safely ashore.

IF YOU HAVE ANY DOUBTS ABOUT WHAT TO TAKE ASK THE PEOPLE YOU'LL BE SAILING WITH.

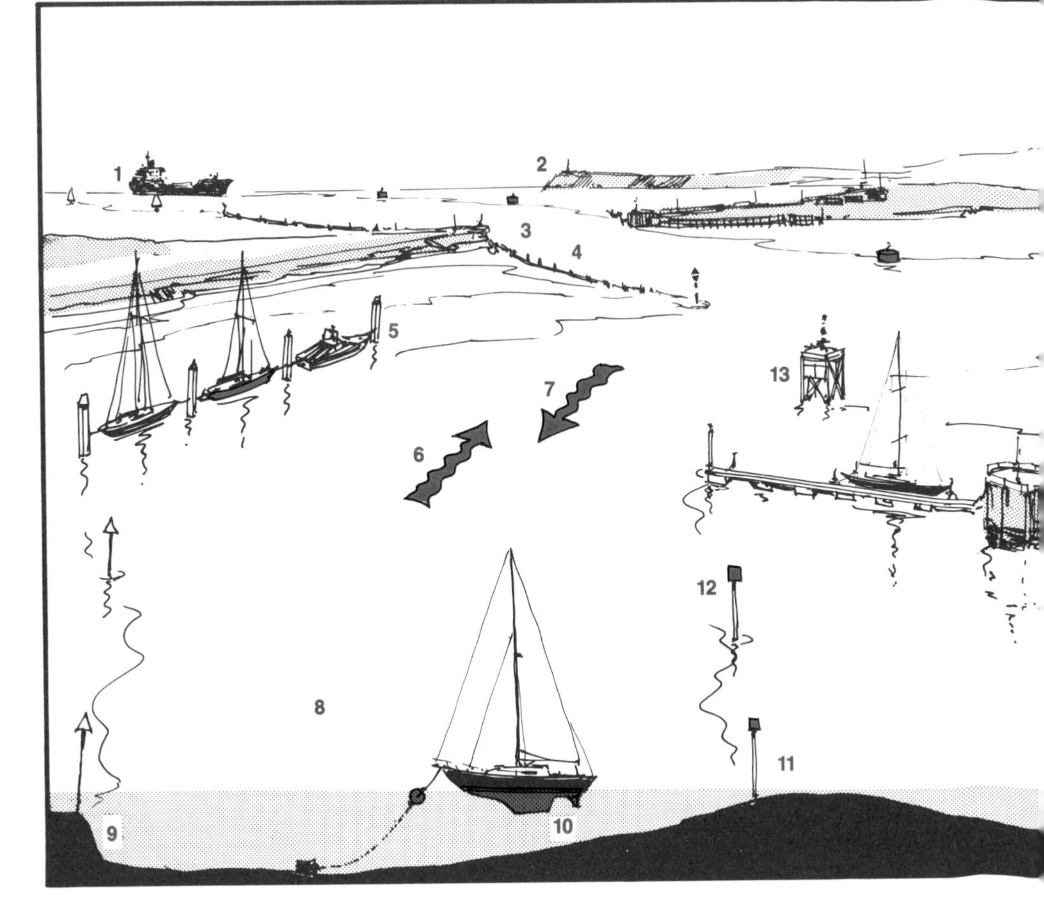

HARBOUR TERMS

Harbours and coastlines abound with strangely named objects and these two pages might help explain what the skipper is talking about.

1. **FAIRWAY**
   Main channel into the harbour.

2. **HEADLAND**
   Prominent land sticking out into the sea.

3. **HARBOUR ENTRANCE**
   Often there are traffic laws to be obeyed.

4. **BREAKWATER, GROYNE, TRAINING BANK**
   Obstruction used to protect the land from the sea.

5. **PILE MOORING**
   Posts driven into the seabed to tie-up to.

6. **EBB**
   When the tide is going out.

7. **FLOOD OR FLOW**
   When the tide is coming in.

8. **CHANNEL**
   Deep water route.

9. **'STEEP TO' CHANNEL EDGE**
   Bottom gets deep quickly.

10. **SHELVING**
    Steep or gentle. How the bottom slopes.

11. **SHOAL OR SHALLOWS**

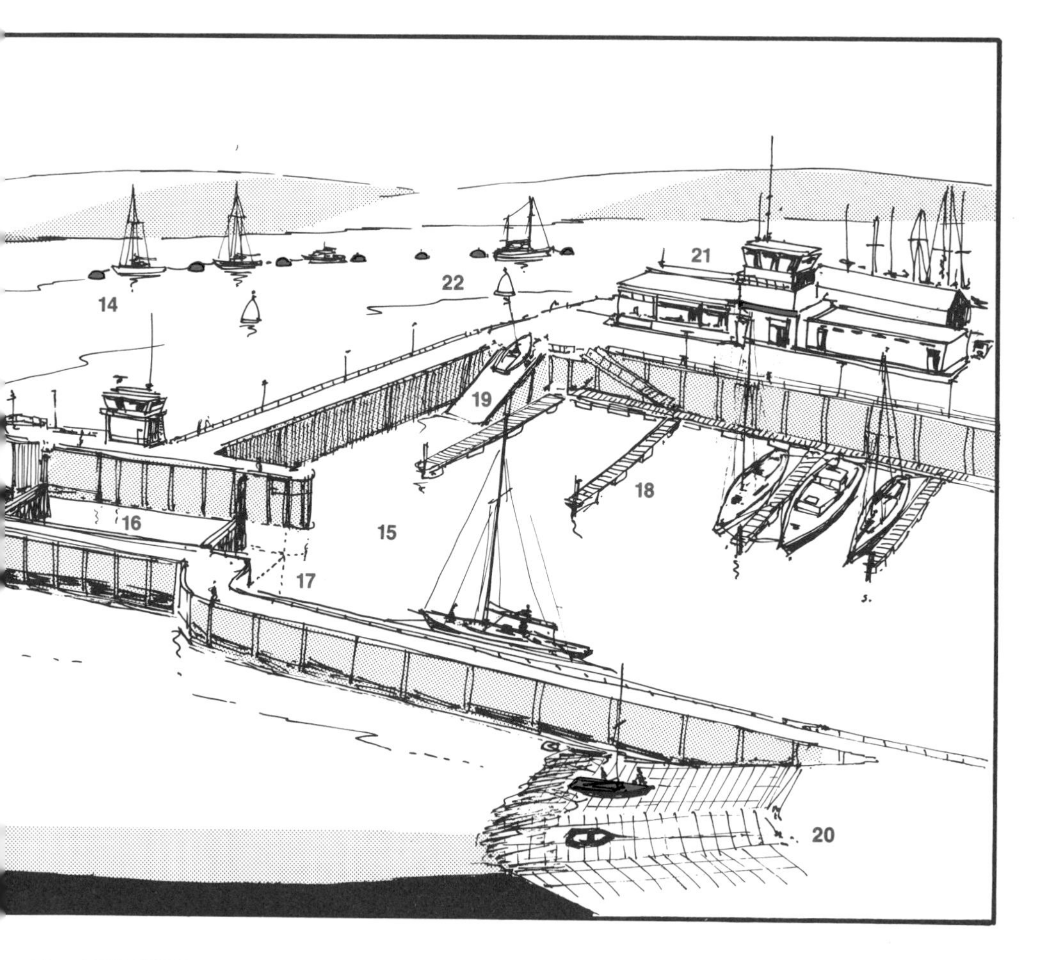

12. BEACON
Navigation mark not always lit.

13. DOLPHIN
Structure used as a navigation mark.

14. MOORING BUOYS
If laid in a line they are called TROTS.

15. MARINA
Enclosed area where boats are 'parked'.

16. LOCK
Used to keep the water level in the marina constant, while still letting boats in and out.

17. CILL
Sometimes instead of a lock a cill or dam is used to keep enough water in the marina.

18. PONTOON
Floating platform to moor boats to.

19. SLIPWAY
Ramp to launch boats.

20. HARD
Solid ground to launch small boats from.

21. CHANDLER
Shop that sells boating equipment.

22. NAVIGATION BUOYS
Buoys used to mark the edge of channels (see back cover).

NAUTICAL TERMS

'PORT' and 'STARBOARD' are often confused – this little saying might help.

"The captain *LEFT* his *RED PORT* wine behind"

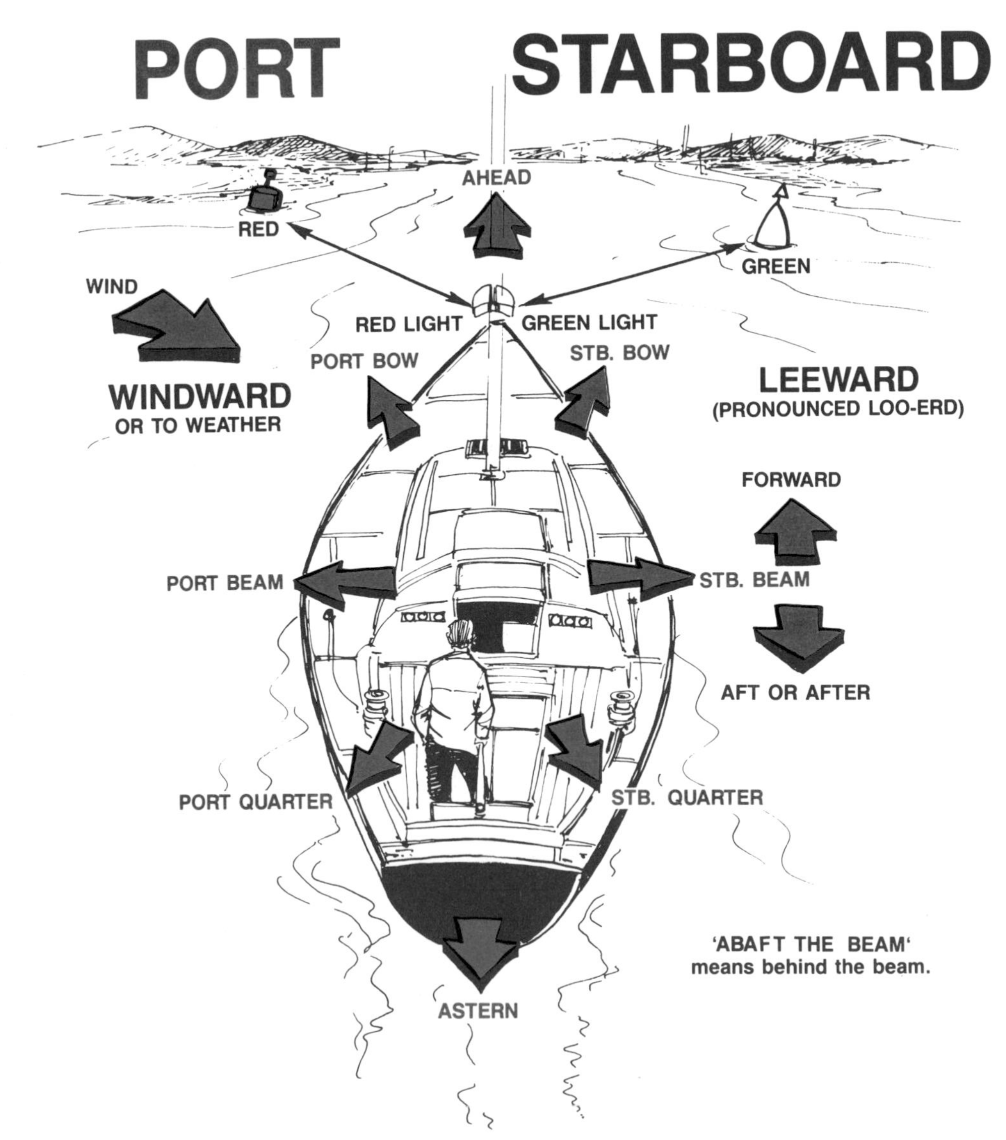

RIGS AND BOATS

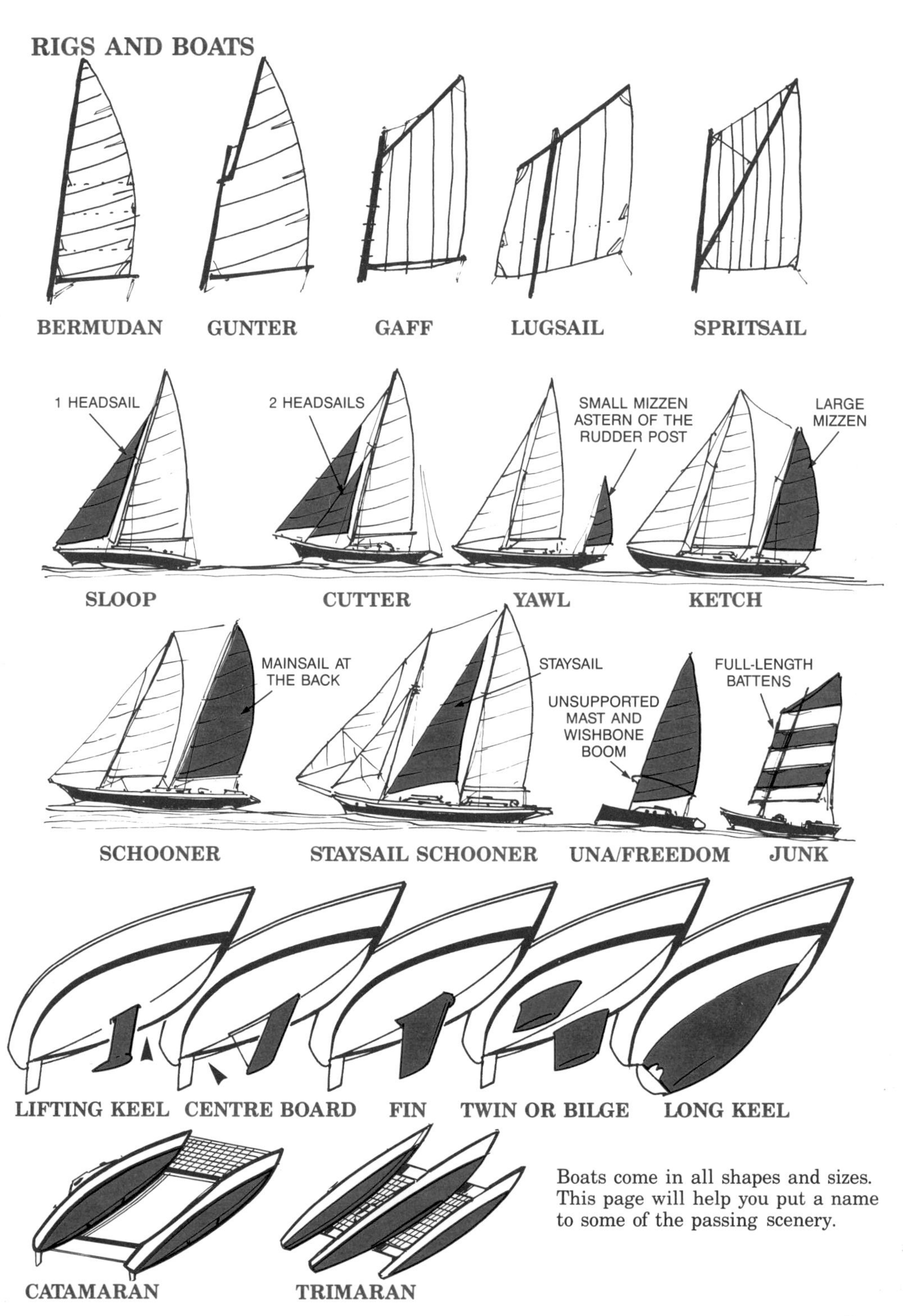

Boats come in all shapes and sizes. This page will help you put a name to some of the passing scenery.

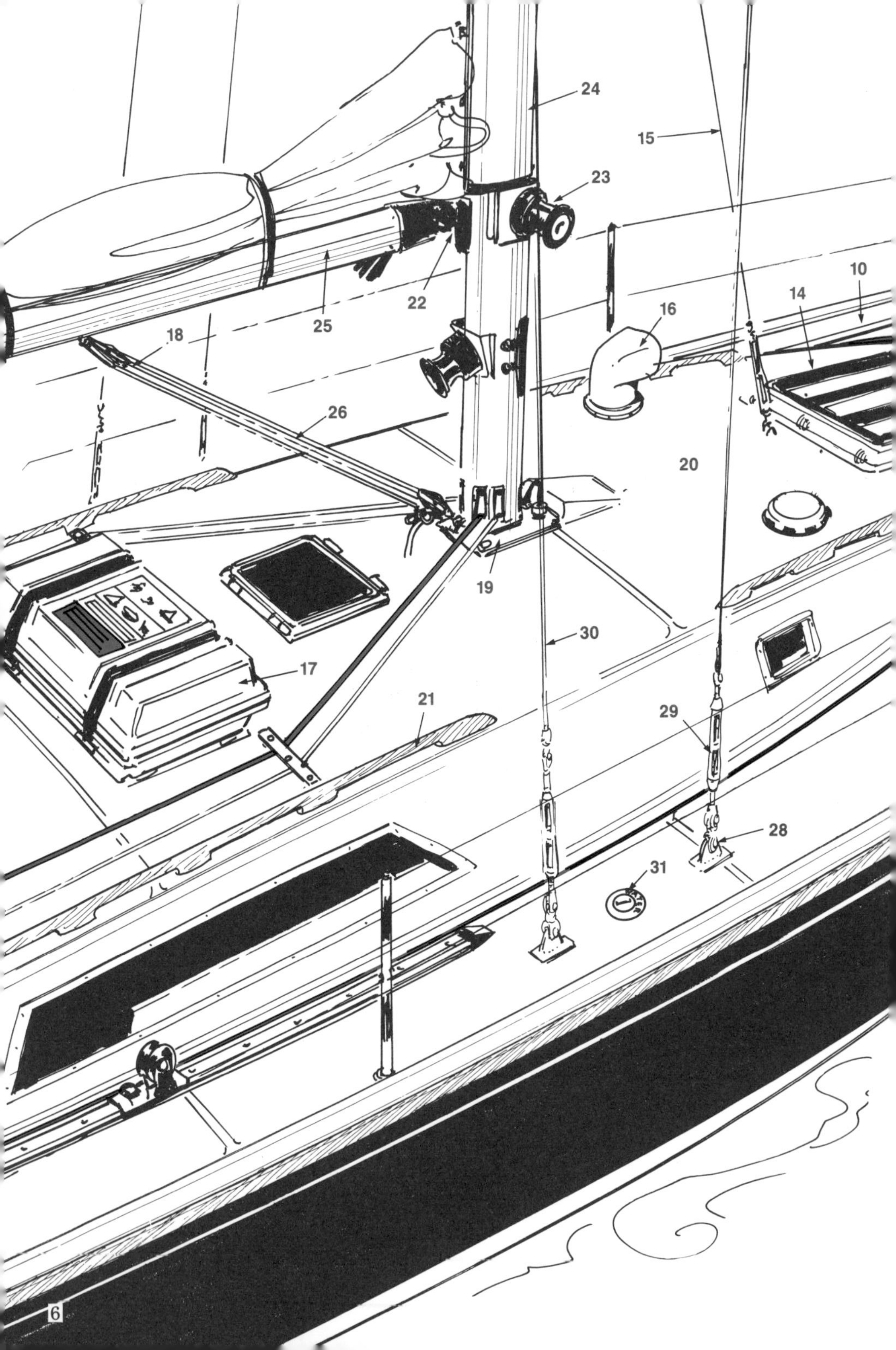
24
15
23
25
22
10
14
16
18
26
20
19
30
17
21
29
28
31

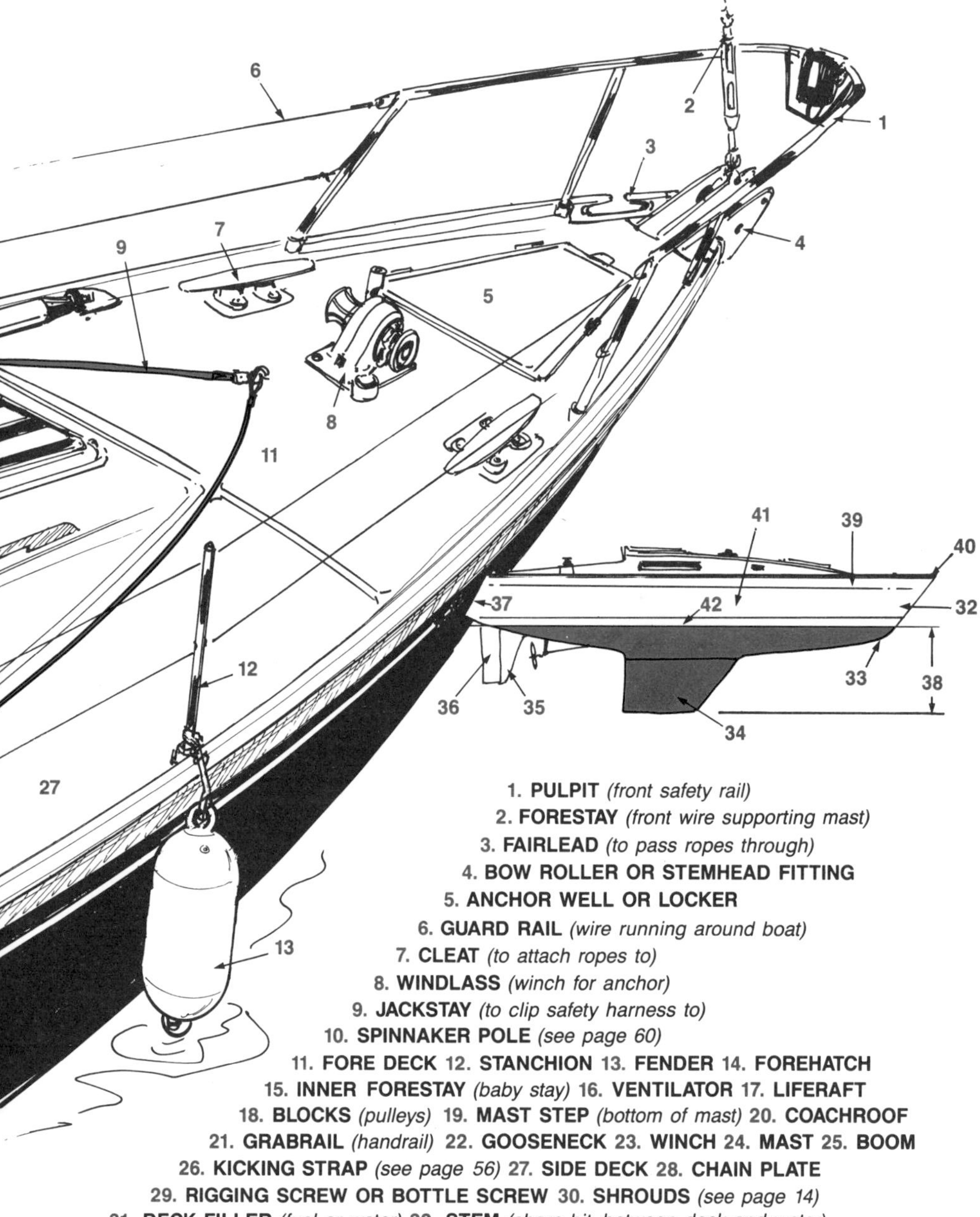

1. **PULPIT** *(front safety rail)*
2. **FORESTAY** *(front wire supporting mast)*
3. **FAIRLEAD** *(to pass ropes through)*
4. **BOW ROLLER OR STEMHEAD FITTING**
5. **ANCHOR WELL OR LOCKER**
6. **GUARD RAIL** *(wire running around boat)*
7. **CLEAT** *(to attach ropes to)*
8. **WINDLASS** *(winch for anchor)*
9. **JACKSTAY** *(to clip safety harness to)*
10. **SPINNAKER POLE** *(see page 60)*

11. **FORE DECK** 12. **STANCHION** 13. **FENDER** 14. **FOREHATCH** 15. **INNER FORESTAY** *(baby stay)* 16. **VENTILATOR** 17. **LIFERAFT** 18. **BLOCKS** *(pulleys)* 19. **MAST STEP** *(bottom of mast)* 20. **COACHROOF** 21. **GRABRAIL** *(handrail)* 22. **GOOSENECK** 23. **WINCH** 24. **MAST** 25. **BOOM** 26. **KICKING STRAP** *(see page 56)* 27. **SIDE DECK** 28. **CHAIN PLATE** 29. **RIGGING SCREW OR BOTTLE SCREW** 30. **SHROUDS** *(see page 14)* 31. **DECK FILLER** *(fuel or water)* 32. **STEM** *(sharp bit between deck and water)* 33. **FOREFOOT** *(where stem and keel meet)* 34. **KEEL** 35. **SKEG** 36. **RUDDER** 37. **STERN** *(back)* 38. **DRAFT** *(depth of water of 'what she draws')* 39. **CAVITA LINE** *(decorative line)* 40. **BOW** *(front)* 41. **TOPSIDES** *(between water and deck)* 42. **BOOT TOP** *(painted band just above water)*

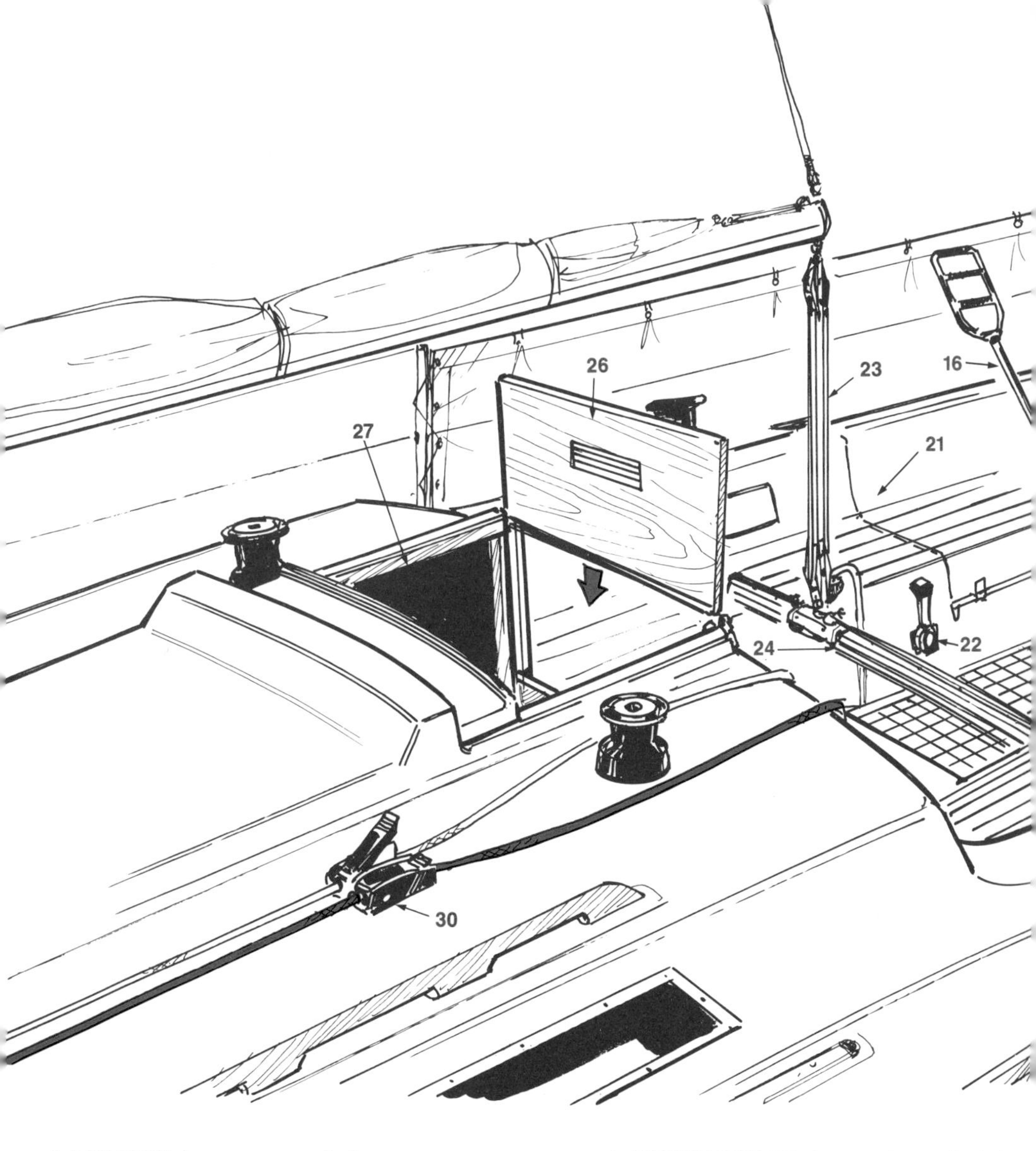

1. **DAN BUOY** *(emergency marker)*

2. **LIFE BUOY** *(see page 28)*

3. **KEDGE ANCHOR** *(secondary anchor)*

4. **PUSHPIT** *(rear safety rail)*

5. **AFTER DECK**

6. **DODGERS** *(to keep spray out)*

7. **STERN LOCKER**

8. **FAIRLEAD** *(to pass ropes through)*

9. **DINGHY PAINTER** *(rope to tie-up dinghy)*

10. **THWART** *(seat)*

11. **BAILER** *(to bail out water)*

12. **ROWLOCK** *('rollock')*

13. **TRANSOM** *(flat back of boat)*

14. **DINGHY OR TENDER**

15. **TILLER**

16. **TILLER EXTENSION**

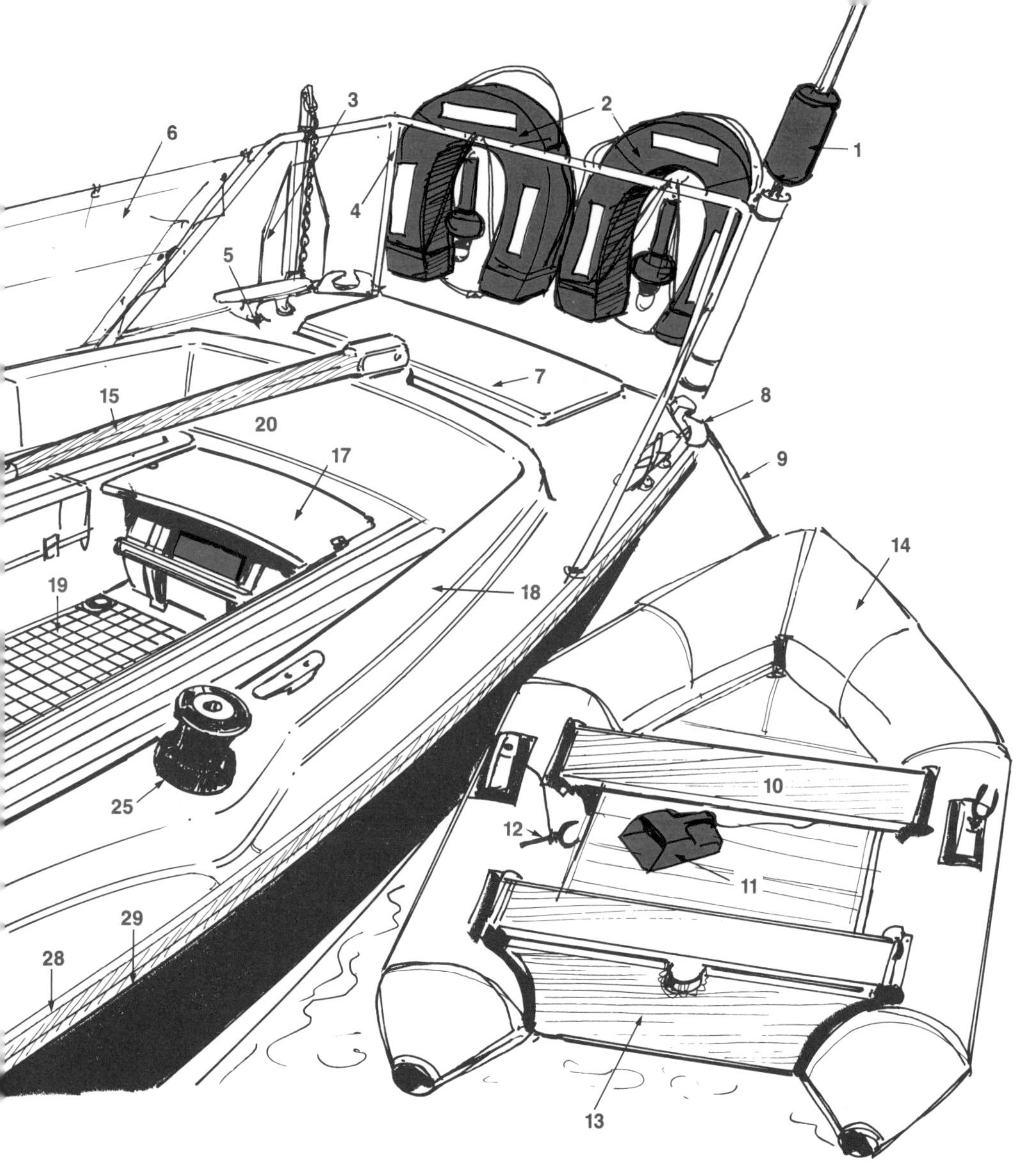

17. **LIFE RAFT STOWAGE** *(not always here)*

18. **COAMING**

19. **COCKPIT SOLE** *(floor)*

20. **COCKPIT**

21. **COCKPIT LOCKER**

22. **ENGINE CONTROLS** *(see page 13)*

23. **MAIN SHEET** *(see page 56)*

24. **MAIN SHEET TRACK**

25. **SHEET WINCH**

26. **WASH BOARDS** *(drop-in boards)*

27. **COMPANIONWAY** *(main entrance)*

28. **TOE RAIL OR GUNWALE**
('gunnel' — top edge of hull)

29. **RUBBING STRAKE** *(bumper)*

30. **JAMMERS** *(see page 34)*

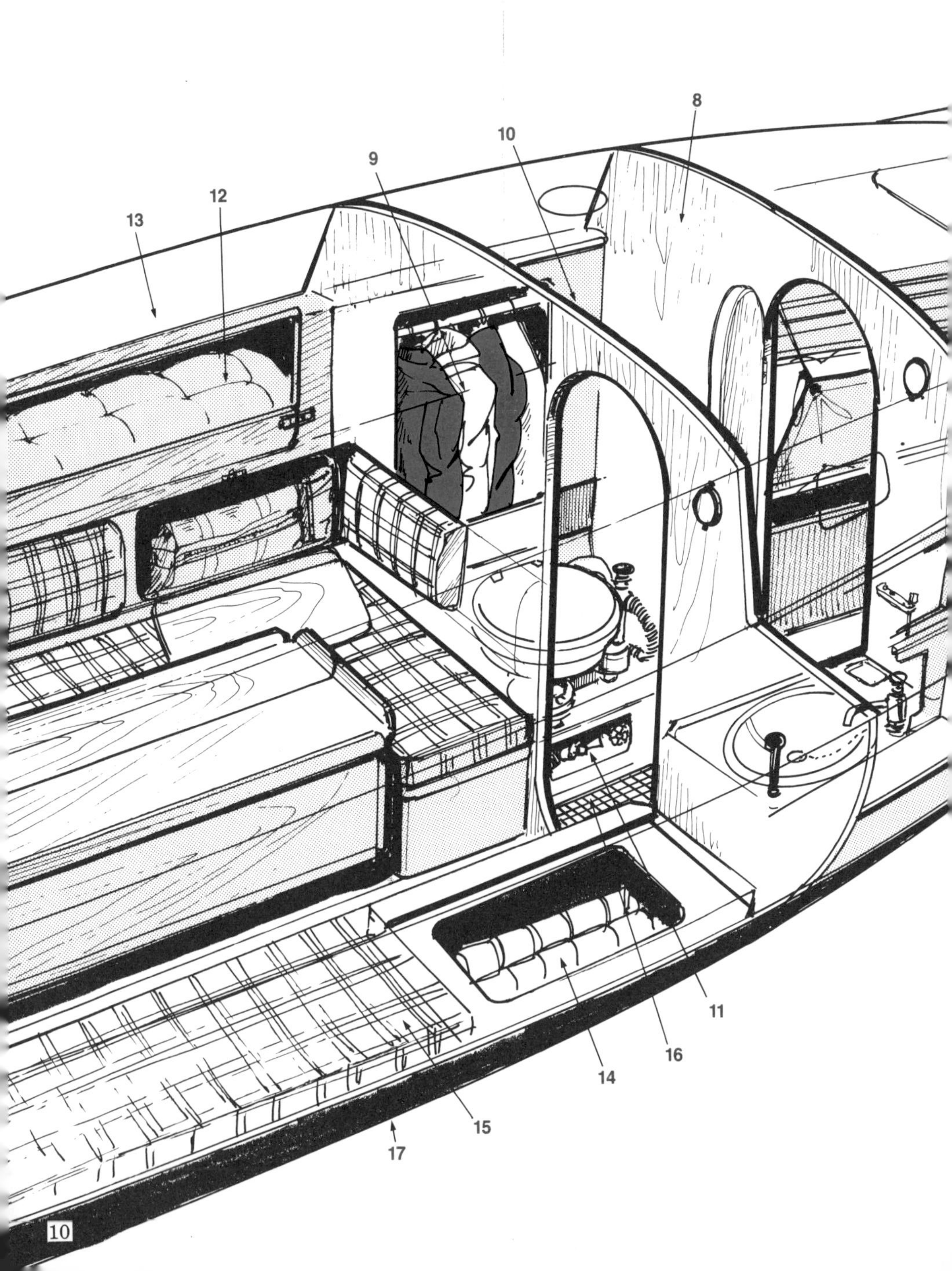
8
10
9
12
13
11
16
14
15
17

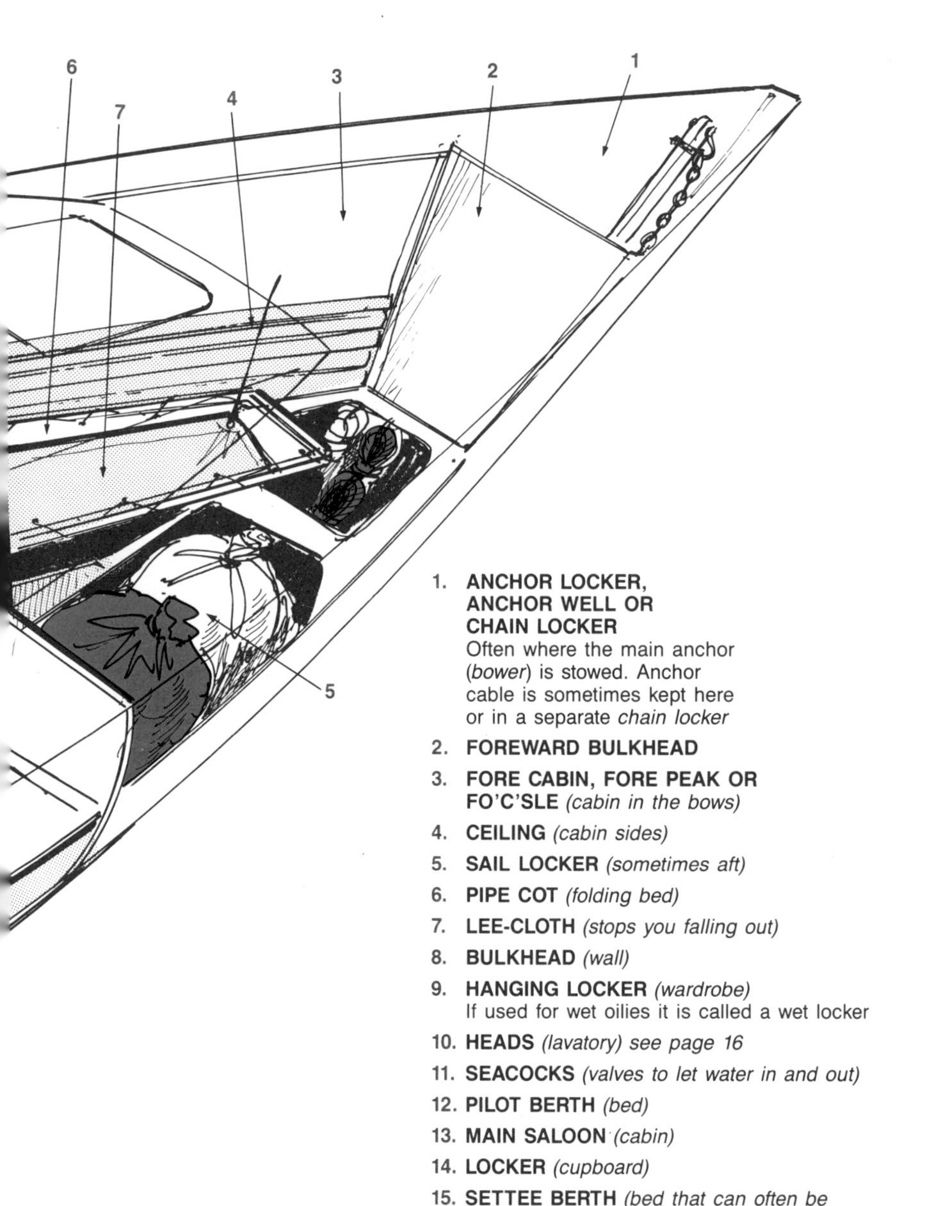

1. **ANCHOR LOCKER, ANCHOR WELL OR CHAIN LOCKER**
   Often where the main anchor (*bower*) is stowed. Anchor cable is sometimes kept here or in a separate *chain locker*
2. **FOREWARD BULKHEAD**
3. **FORE CABIN, FORE PEAK OR FO'C'SLE** *(cabin in the bows)*
4. **CEILING** *(cabin sides)*
5. **SAIL LOCKER** *(sometimes aft)*
6. **PIPE COT** *(folding bed)*
7. **LEE-CLOTH** *(stops you falling out)*
8. **BULKHEAD** *(wall)*
9. **HANGING LOCKER** *(wardrobe)*
   If used for wet oilies it is called a wet locker
10. **HEADS** *(lavatory) see page 16*
11. **SEACOCKS** *(valves to let water in and out)*
12. **PILOT BERTH** *(bed)*
13. **MAIN SALOON** *(cabin)*
14. **LOCKER** *(cupboard)*
15. **SETTEE BERTH** *(bed that can often be converted into a double by lowering the table)*
16. **CABIN SOLE** *(floor)*
17. **BILGE** *(where the bottom of the boat joins the sides or the space under the sole)*

1. **COMPANIONWAY** *(entrance to cabin)*
2. **WASH BOARDS** *(drop-in boards)*
3. **FIRE EXTINGUISHER** *(see page 29)*
4. **FLARES** *Not always here (see page 31)*
5. **COMPANIONWAY STEPS**
6. **FIRE BLANKET** *(see page 29)*
7. **QUARTER BERTH** *(bed)* Sometimes a small cabin — quarter cabin or after cabin.
8. **DECK HEAD** *(ceiling)*
9. **CHART TABLE** *(navigation area)*
10. **GALLEY** *(kitchen)*
11. **ICE-BOX**
12. **GIMBALLED STOVE** *(Swings with ship's movement see page 17)*

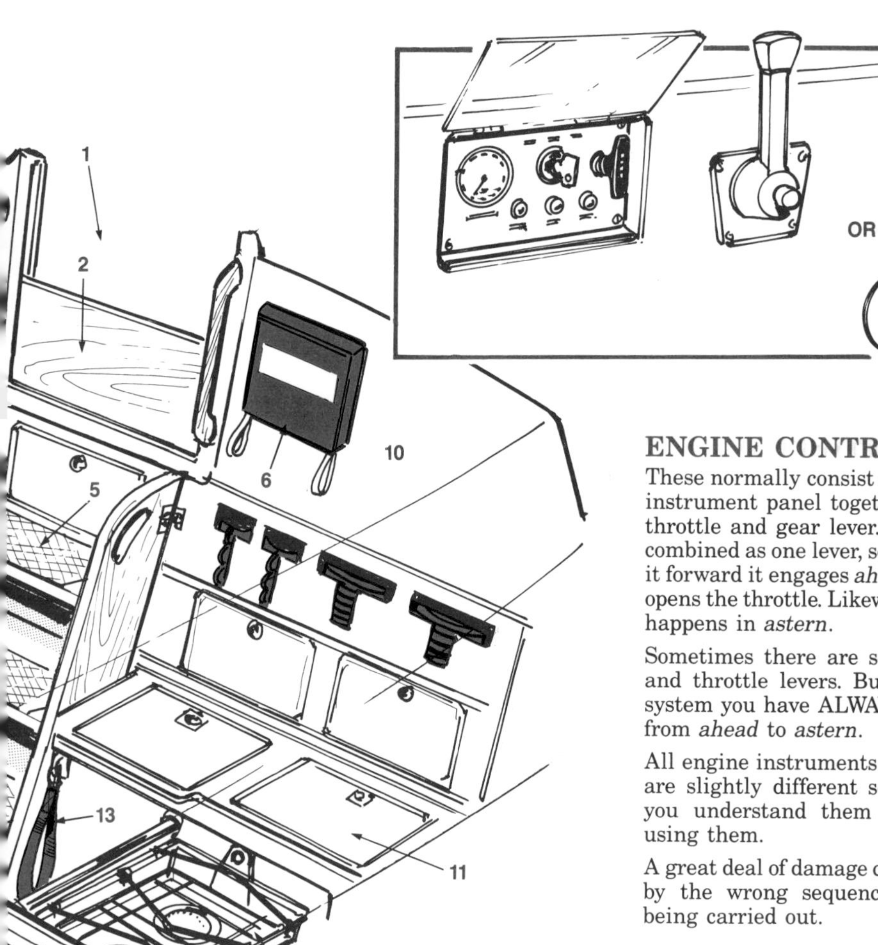

ENGINE CONTROLS

These normally consist of the engine instrument panel together with the throttle and gear lever. This can be combined as one lever, so as you push it forward it engages *ahead* and then opens the throttle. Likewise the same happens in *astern*.

Sometimes there are separate gear and throttle levers. But, whichever system you have ALWAYS go gently from *ahead* to *astern*.

All engine instruments and controls are slightly different so make sure you understand them fully before using them.

A great deal of damage can be caused by the wrong sequence of actions being carried out.

13. **SAFETY STRAP FOR COOK**

14. **HALF-BULKHEADS**

15. **GRAB RAILS**

16. **LOCKERS**
(cupboards)

17. **CABIN SOLE**
(floor)

RIGGING

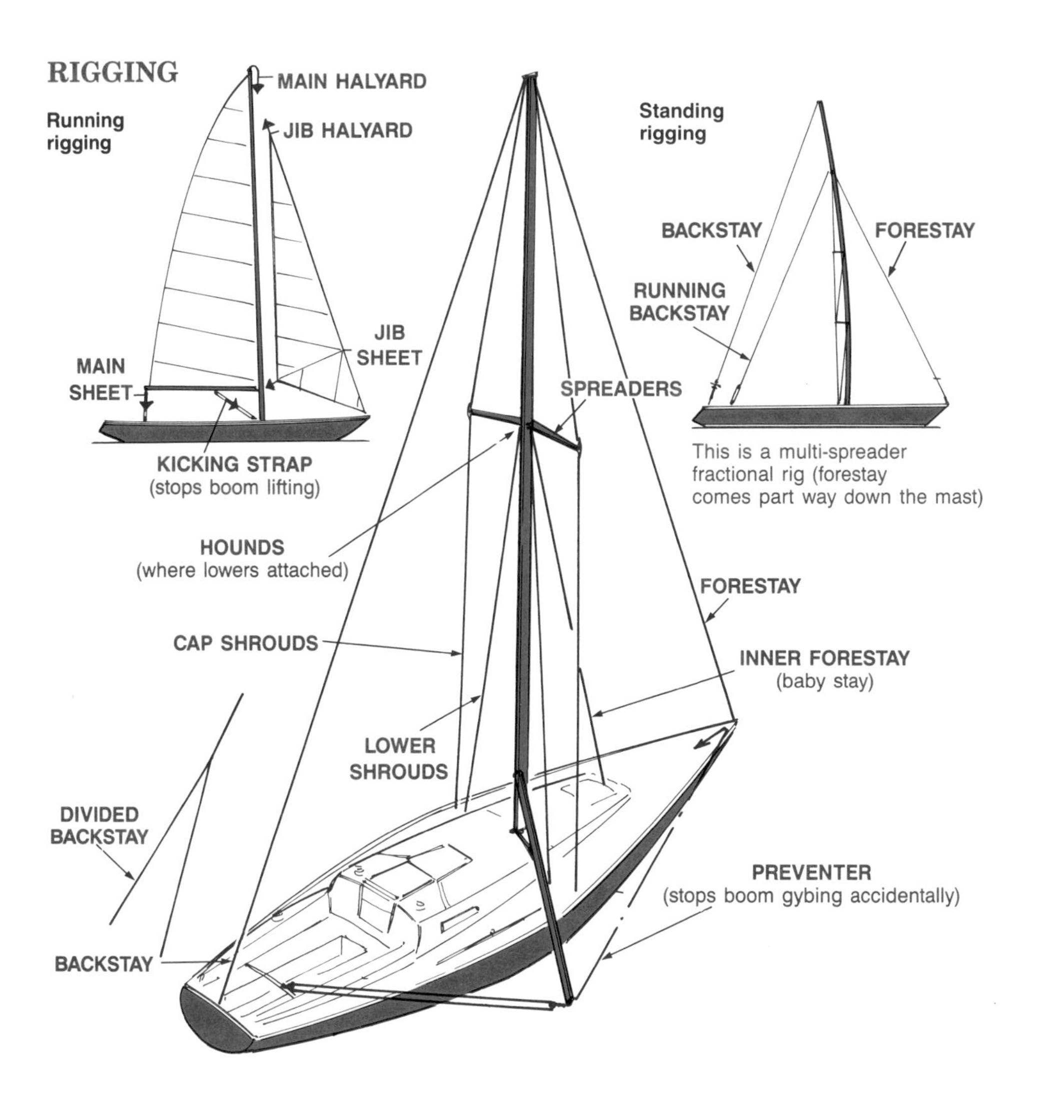

All the lines on a boat that are fixed to the mast in some way are called the rigging. Those which move to control the sails are called the RUNNING RIGGING and those that hold the mast up are called the STANDING RIGGING.
RUNNING RIGGING is normally rope but on larger boats flexible wire is also used.
STANDING RIGGING is often made of wire and on some boats can be adjusted to alter the shape of the sail by bending the mast.

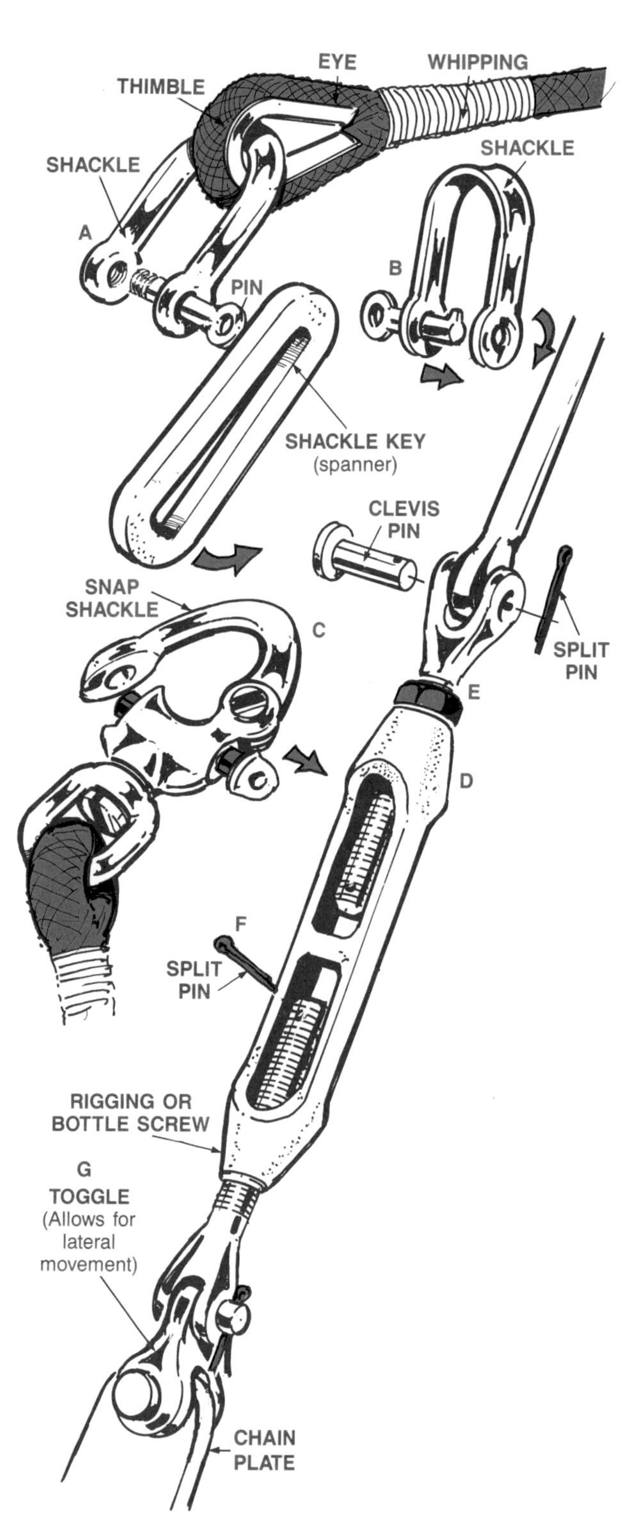

RUNNING RIGGING

Rigging lines are usually attached to other things (such as sails) by some form of fastening called a SHACKLE.
These come in various sizes and open in a variety of ways.

(A) The most common type has a screw-in pin, which can be tightened with a slotted spanner called a SHACKLE KEY (often these are incorporated in sailor's knives).

(B) Another type simply has a 'push and turn' keyhole pin.

(C) Spring loaded SNAP SHACKLES open in several different ways some have triggers, but the most common have a pull-out pin.

STANDING RIGGING

The tension in the standing rigging is usually adjusted by turning a RIGGING SCREW (D). This has a left and right handed thread so each turn either tightens or loosens the rigging wire. Once adjusted, the rigging screw is locked in position by a locknut (E), split pin (F) or locking wire.

Any signs of damage or looseness in these fittings must be reported to the skipper.

The rigging wire is attached to the rigging screw with a clevis pin and split pin. These are usually taped over to stop them tearing sails.

The rigging screw is connected to the boat via some form of toggle (G) which allows for some degree of movement.

The toggle in turn is fixed to a chain plate or strong U bolt. Again any signs of wear in these components should be reported.

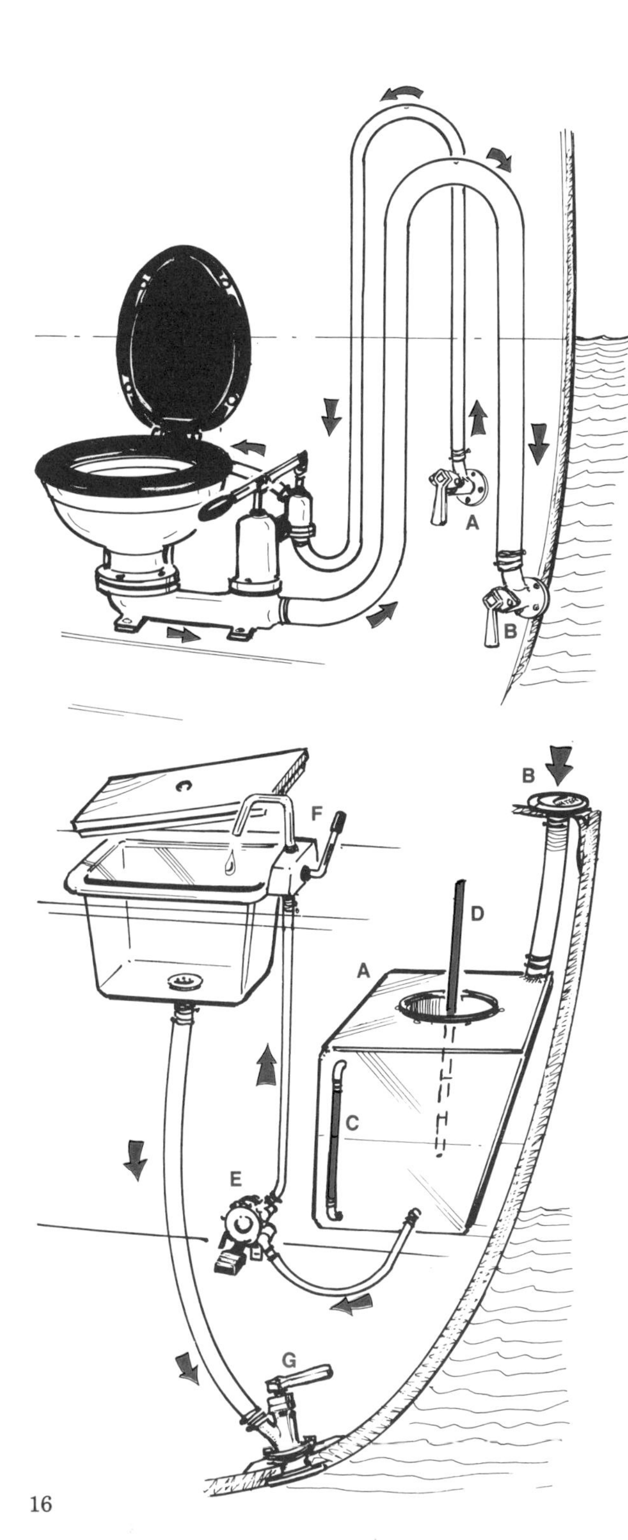

WATER – the heads

On a boat, the lavatory is called 'the heads', as in the past seamen used to use the front of the boat or 'head' as a toilet. Today, the marine W.C.'s vary quite considerably in design and operation, so, make sure you understand how to use the one on your boat.

Basically, they all suck in sea water through a seacock (valve) (**A**), flush the bowl and pump it out through another seacock (**B**) (or into a holding tank).

Only things which have passed through the body and moderate amounts of lavatory paper can be successfully flushed away.

So, women using sanitary towels should also take along a supply of disposal bags.

To prevent syphoning, the pipes carrying water to and from the lavatory rise above the water level and the seacocks are turned off at sea, when the system is not being used.

FRESH WATER

All fresh water is carried in tanks (**A**), which are filled from the deck (**B**) and the levels are checked either by a sight-tube (**C**) or dip stick (**D**).

Water gets to the sink via a footpump (**E**), hand pump (**F**) or an electric pump, whose switch often looks like a tap.

Waste water drains out through another seacock (**G**) or into a holding tank which can be pumped out later.

DO NOT WASTE WATER.

GAS

Bottled gas is the main fuel used for cooking and can be very dangerous.

Normally, the bottle lives in a draining, cockpit locker which lets any escaping gas leak overboard.

A STRICT SEQUENCE *MUST* BE USED TO STOP GAS ESCAPING

TO TURN ON

1. **MAKE SURE ALL TAPS ARE CLOSED. ASK HOW THEY ALL WORK.**
2. **TURN ON AT THE BOTTLE (A)**
3. **TURN ON THE MAIN COCK (B)**
4. **LIGHT THE MATCH**
5. **TURN ON THE BURNER**
6. **DISPOSE OF THE MATCH SAFELY**

TO TURN OFF:-

If you are going to use the stove again soon:

1. **TURN OFF THE MAIN COCK (B)**
2. **LET THE GAS BURN OUT**
3. **SHUT THE BURNER TAP**

If you have finished with the stove

1. **TURN OFF AT THE BOTTLE**
2. **LET THE GAS BURN OUT OF THE SYSTEM**
3. **SHUT OFF THE MAIN COCK**
4. **SHUT OFF THE BURNER TAP**

Liquid petroleum gas is heavier than air so, any small amounts that escape, sink into the bilge and might *accumulate into an explosive mixture*.

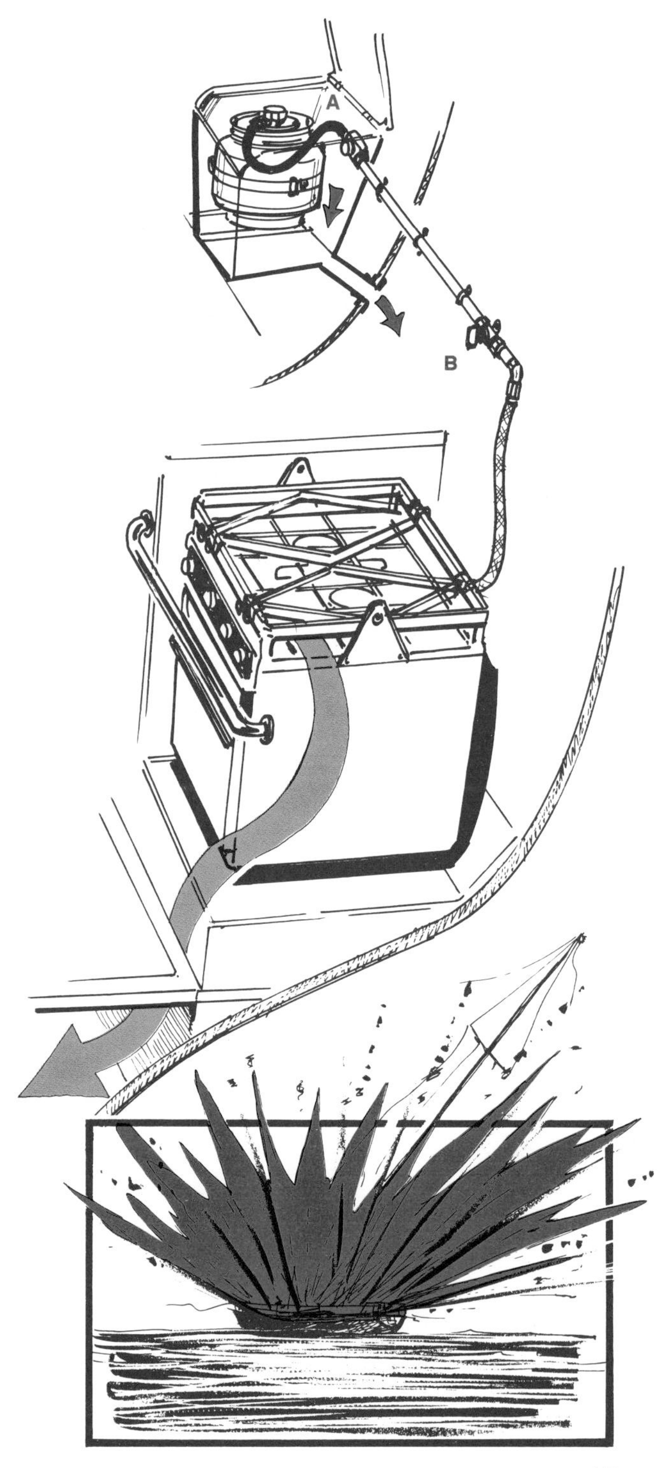

LIVING AFLOAT

Cooking This is awkward on a boat due to the very limited space and constant movement. In rough weather, the cook and his utensils need to be firmly wedged-in. The dangers of hot spilled liquids can be reduced by wearing oilskin trousers and boots and only part fill any containers that are used.
The sink is a very good place to hold mugs while pouring out hot drinks as any spills go straight down the drain.

Sleeping Boats may provide sleeping bags or you can take your own. All bunks should be equipped with 'lee-cloths' to stop you falling out in the event of heavy weather. Although usually they aren't needed and the gentle movement of the boat rocks you to sleep.

Tidiness All gear needs to be kept in its correct place so *everyone* knows where to find it. This goes equally for the humble teaspoon as well as emergency equipment.

Often lists of contents are displayed inside locker lids to help with this.
Personal gear should be tidied away to avoid accidents and to stop it getting soaked in rough weather.
A bag which you can live out of saves unpacking and gives the contents a little extra protection from the wet.
Try not to drip onto bunks when moving about in wet oilskins and avoid leaving your gear just where it fell!

GOLDEN RULES FOR LIFE AFLOAT

Be clean and tidy – wipe up any spills straight away and pack everything away neatly.
Don't leave lights on as this wastes the boat's limited battery power.
Don't waste water as only a certain amount of fresh water can be carried aboard and if its wasted, valuable sailing time has to be used up refilling the tanks.
Be tolerant.

DO'S AND DON'TS WHEN MOORED ALONGSIDE

DO – Tidy the boat up before going ashore

DO – Make sure all the mooring warps and fenders are secured properly (see page 33) and the ends of lines coiled neatly.

DO – Look aloft to make sure that lines won't knock against the mast all night.

DO – Put the sail cover on to protect the mainsail.

DO – Coil and stow the sheets

DO – Look around the boat and report any signs of wear and tear to the skipper.

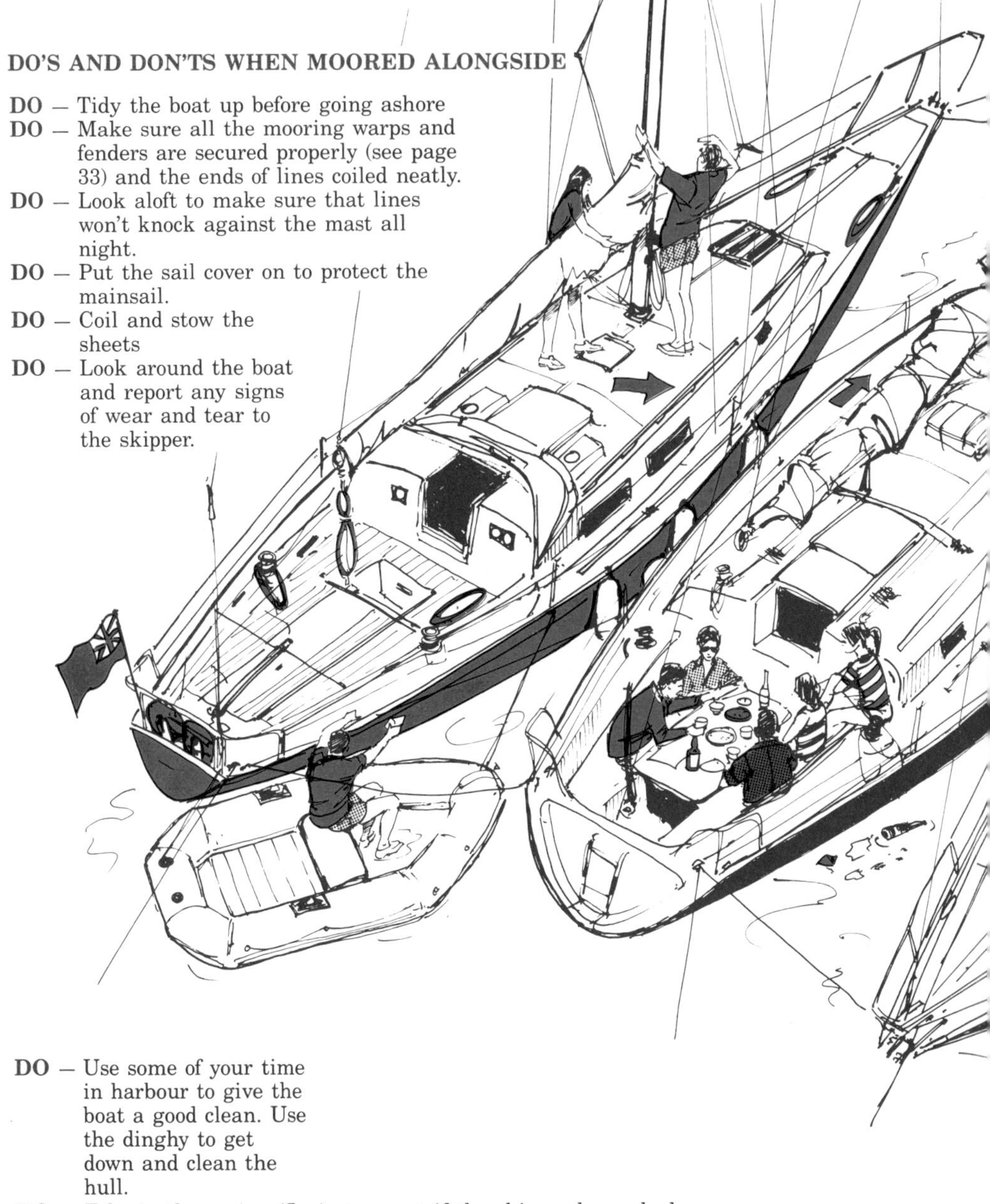

DO – Use some of your time in harbour to give the boat a good clean. Use the dinghy to get down and clean the hull.

DO – Take in the ensign (flag) at sunset if the skipper has asked you to do so. (It's a custom that the ensign isn't flown in harbour between the hours of 2100 – 0800).

DO – Secure the dinghy so it won't obstruct other people and so it doesn't bump the boat all night.

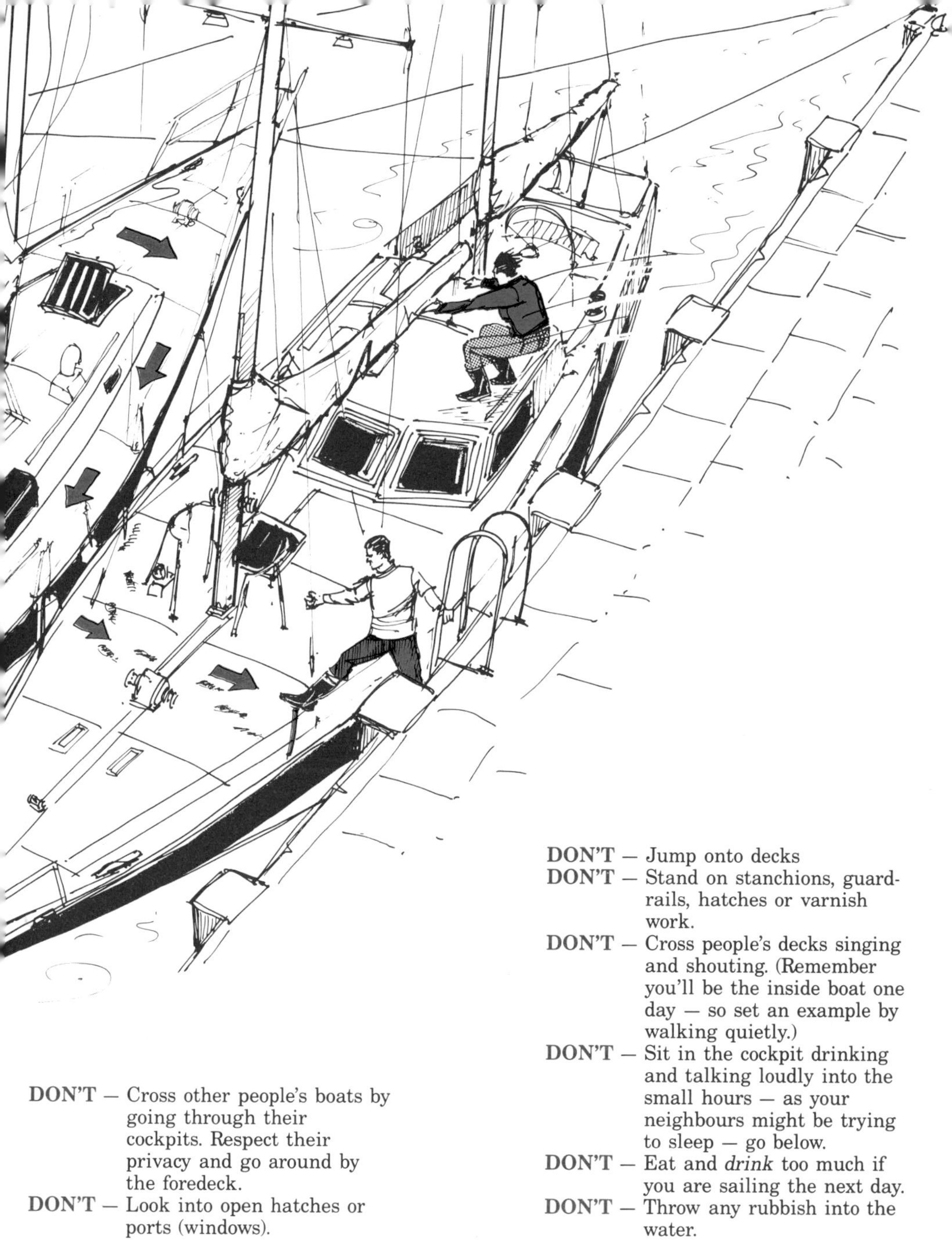

DON'T – Cross other people's boats by going through their cockpits. Respect their privacy and go around by the foredeck.

DON'T – Look into open hatches or ports (windows).

DON'T – Jump onto decks

DON'T – Stand on stanchions, guard-rails, hatches or varnish work.

DON'T – Cross people's decks singing and shouting. (Remember you'll be the inside boat one day – so set an example by walking quietly.)

DON'T – Sit in the cockpit drinking and talking loudly into the small hours – as your neighbours might be trying to sleep – go below.

DON'T – Eat and *drink* too much if you are sailing the next day.

DON'T – Throw any rubbish into the water.

DINGHIES

Yachts' tenders (dinghies) come in all shapes and sizes and by learning to control them properly you'll add to your enjoyment afloat. *But* used incorrectly they can be very dangerous.

THIS IS AN EXAMPLE OF WHAT YOU SHOULD NOT DO!

Make several trips, rather than overloading the dinghy, as a passing wash could swamp you. Don't stand up and always place stores on the deck *before* trying to leave the dinghy. The dinghy is more stable if secured by the painter (bow rope) rather than just holding on. And, never leave metal rowlocks in when alongside a yacht as they will scratch her hull. Also, try not to let your fingers be squashed between the two boats!

ROWING A dinghy will row easier if she's not overloaded and the weight distributed so she's trimmed level.

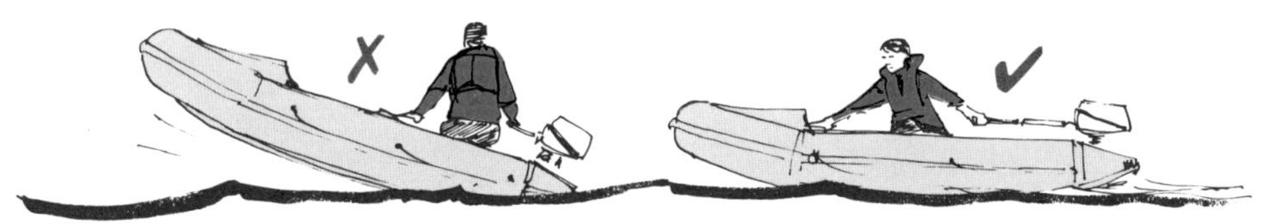

OUTBOARD MOTORS Again, the boat will go better and be more seaworthy if you trim her level. This might mean using an extension on the outboard's tiller and sitting further forward. The boat on the left is dangerous as the wind could flip her over.

USING A DINGHY AT NIGHT
This can be very pleasurable *or* extremely dangerous. Always wear some form of buoyancy, and take the oars as well as the outboard. Take a torch, to warm others you're there and *to find your own boat again!*

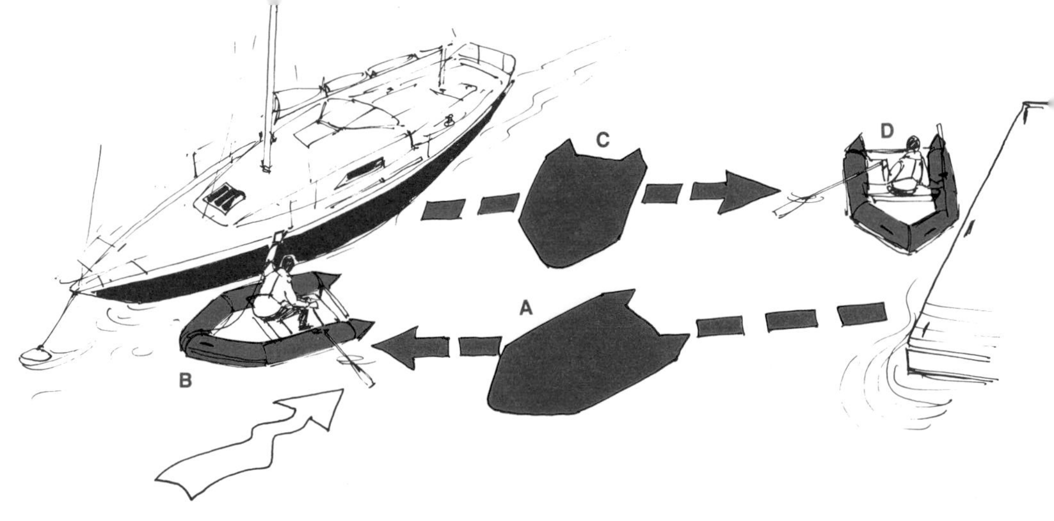

ROWING ACROSS A CURRENT

(A) When rowing out to a yacht you must allow for any tidal stream so, aim well up stream and gradually 'crab' across the current.
(B) Unship the inboard oar (and rowlock) and let the tide ease you back.
(C) When leaving the yacht to go ashore keep the bows facing up into the stream otherwise you'll be swept way downstream.
(D) Unship the inboard oar and 'push' the other one to spin you in alongside. Make fast smartly.

OUTBOARD SAFETY

NEVER, EVER TRY TO START AN OUTBOARD WHEN STANDING IN THE WATER NEXT TO IT.
When it fires it can jump forward and slice into your legs! Row the boat off a good distance from the beach and start the engine when you are safely inside.
Also, beware of the trailing painter fouling the propeller.

ALWAYS CUT THE ENGINE AND TIP IT UP WHEN APPROACHING A BEACH.
This will save the propeller from damaging itself by churning up the sand.
Also, don't let inflatables run up onto a stony beach. Stop in the shallows and unload her there. This will avoid tearing the bottom and the need to use the repair kit and pump you should be carrying.

Moving around the boat safely means always:

(A) Using the windward (uphill) side so, if you fall, you'll fall inboard. It will also keep you away from the sails and let you brace your feet against the cabin sides.

(B) Keeping your body weight low if it's choppy and crawling if it's really rough.

(C) Holding on to something secure and remembering
'It's one hand for you and one hand for the boat!'

BE AWARE OF WHAT'S HAPPENING AROUND YOU
Accidental gybes have killed people and flogging sails have damaged eyes.

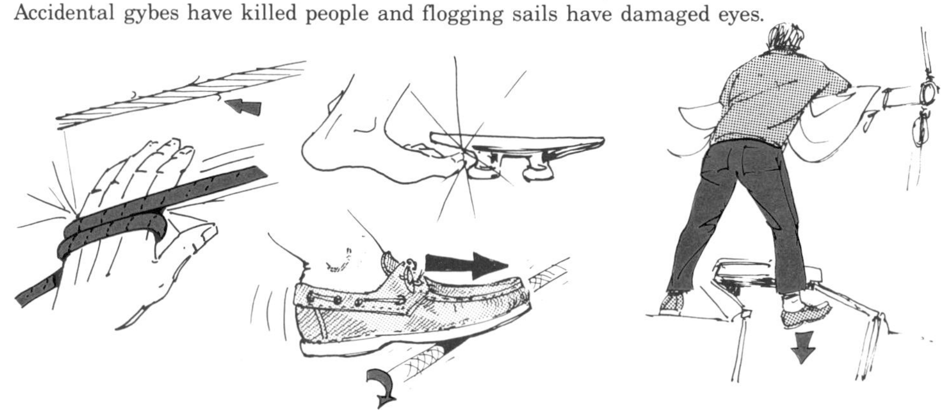

'Fishooks' on wire rope can cut fingers and NEVER put a rope around your hand.
Think where you're putting your feet and try to wear shoes to protect your toes. Ropes and wet sails can make you slip and open hatches can be forgotten about!

WET WEATHER GEAR

A good set of oilies and boots is an expensive investment, but they should last for years. Sailing schools will lend or hire you a set but if you decide to buy, here are some things to look for:-

SAFETY HARNESS

Each crew member should be supplied with a safety harness that can be adjusted to a reasonably tight fit.
Once adjusted it can be easily put on when needed.
ALWAYS WEAR A HARNESS *IF YOU FEEL UNSAFE* OR WHEN THE SKIPPER TELLS YOU TO DO SO.
Don't be influenced by what other crew members are doing.

There are various types of spring clips but make sure yours works and is clipped onto something strong.

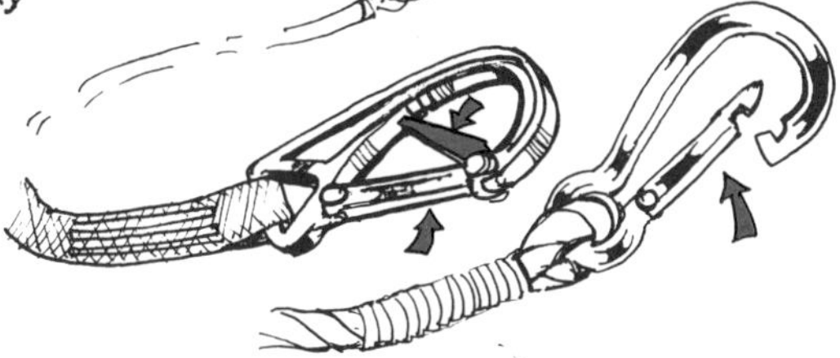

The lifeline can be clipped on to any suitable fitting that is securely bolted to the deck. If it is too large, clip it back on itself but try to avoid fittings on the edge of the boat like stanchions and lifelines. The idea is to clip on *uphill* so if you fall, you fall *into* the boat and in heavy weather ALWAYS clip on *before* leaving the cabin or cockpit.

LIFEJACKETS

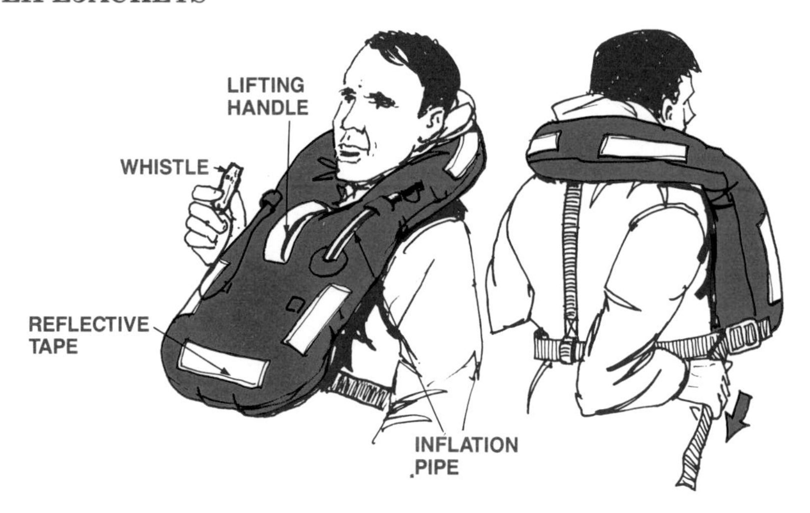

Each crew member must have a life jacket and know how to use it. They vary slightly in design, but basically go over the head and are held on with straps that are buckled or tied at the sides. Some inflate automatically but most have to be blowm up by mouth.

IN THE WATER

By adopting this position in the water the body loses less heat and the hands keep the spray out of the nose and mouth.

OTHER FORMS OF BUOYANCY

Buoyancy aids **(A)** are floating waistcoats normally worn by dinghy sailors.
Float coats **(B)** are jackets with some form of buoyancy built into them.
Both are comfortable to wear but neither one is as good as a lifejacket in an emergency.

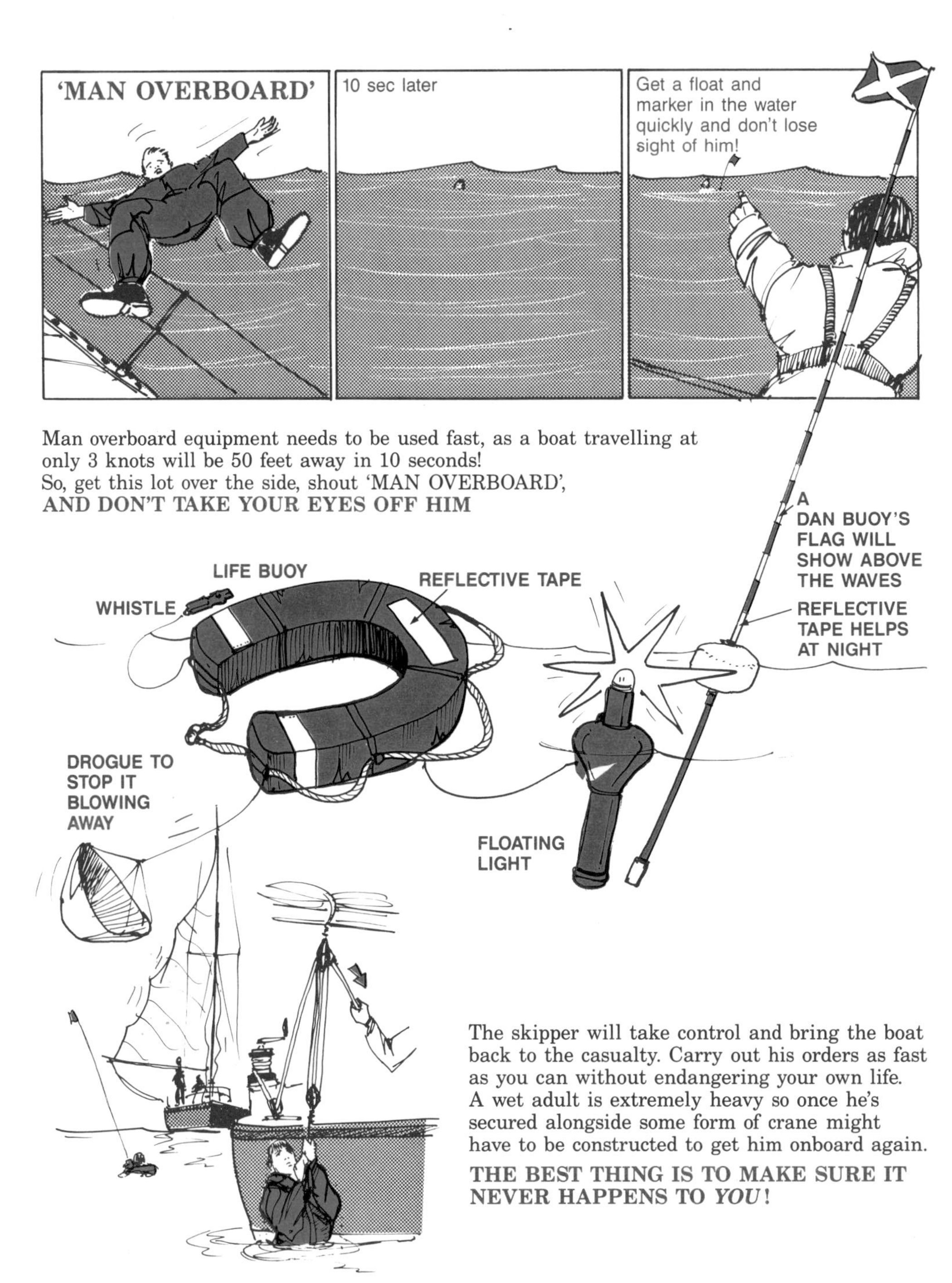

Man overboard equipment needs to be used fast, as a boat travelling at only 3 knots will be 50 feet away in 10 seconds!
So, get this lot over the side, shout 'MAN OVERBOARD',
AND DON'T TAKE YOUR EYES OFF HIM

The skipper will take control and bring the boat back to the casualty. Carry out his orders as fast as you can without endangering your own life. A wet adult is extremely heavy so once he's secured alongside some form of crane might have to be constructed to get him onboard again.

THE BEST THING IS TO MAKE SURE IT NEVER HAPPENS TO *YOU*!

FIRE

Remember;

FIRE NEEDS:- HEAT, FUEL AND OXYGEN cut out any one and the fire goes out.
But, as always prevention is better so:-
NEVER — smoke while refuelling or in a bunk
NEVER — discard matches carelessly
NEVER — let oil, waste paper etc accumulate
ALWAYS REPORT SMELLS OF GAS and use the cooking stores properly (see page 17)

FIRE EXTINGUISHERS

There are two main types: **DRY POWDER** (colour coded blue) and **HALON or BCF** (colour coded green). Both can be used on any fire onboard a boat.
LEARN HOW TO USE THEM CORRECTLY, AND USE THEM FAST.

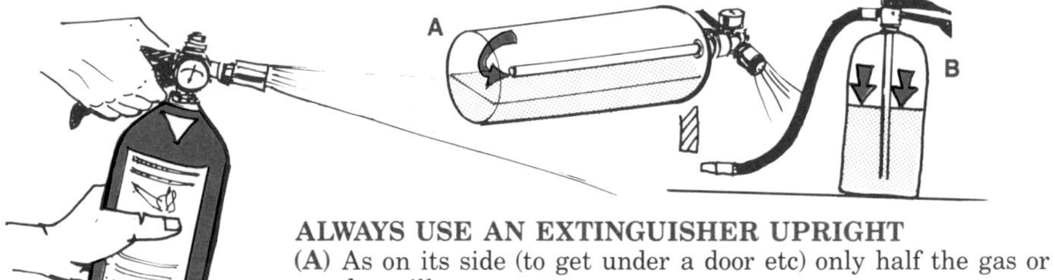

ALWAYS USE AN EXTINGUISHER UPRIGHT
(A) As on its side (to get under a door etc) only half the gas or powder will come out.
(B) The tube nozzle type can be used upright yet still get to awkward places.

FIRE BLANKETS

Fire blankets (or wet dish cloths) can be used to smother a galley fire.

- Hold it like this to protect your hands and push it over the flames.
- If a person's clothes catch fire;

1. Push them over so the flames rise away from the face
2. Smother the flames *away* from the face

SMOKE

If the modern plastics in a boat catch fire they can give off VERY poisonous fumes.
SO, NEVER BREATHE IN THE SMOKE.

VHF RADIO DISTRESS CALL

A distress call is sent when there is *GRAVE AND IMMINENT* danger to a vessel or person and *IMMEDIATE ASSISTANCE* is required.

HOW TO SEND A DISTRESS CALL.

Switch on power, switch on radio, *select CH16*. Turn to high power. Push press-to-transmit switch and speak slowly and distinctly.

Turning on the set etc. can be forgotten in an emergency so make up a reminder card and stick it up near the radio.

- MAYDAY, MAYDAY, MAYDAY.

MAYDAY is the international distress signal.

- This is (yacht name 3 times)
- MAYDAY (yacht's name)

The name and the word yacht helps the searchers know what they are looking for.

- Position (see below)

See below

- Nature of distress
- Any extra information which might help

'I require immediate assistance' and include number of people on board, whether you are going to abandon ship or have fired flares etc.

- Over
- Release transmit switch

'Over' means please reply.

AN URGENCY CALL

An urgency call is used when you have a *very important* message to send covering *safety.*

PAN PAN, PAN PAN, PAN PAN,
Hello all stations (3 times) this is (yacht name 3 times)

- Position
- Nature of urgency
- Assistance required
- Over

The advantage of an urgency call is that it lets the world know you are in some sort of trouble without launching all the rescue services at that moment.

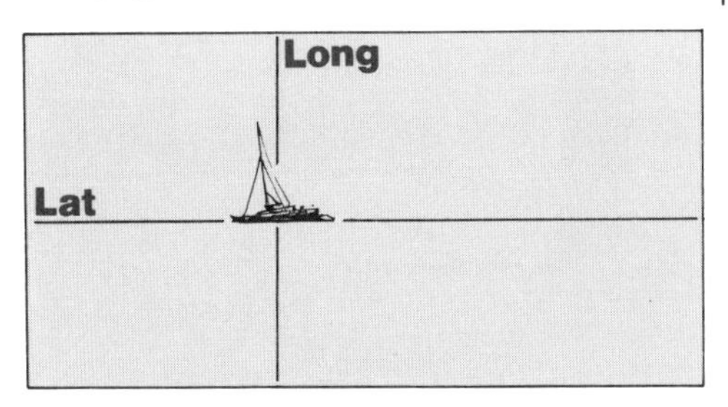

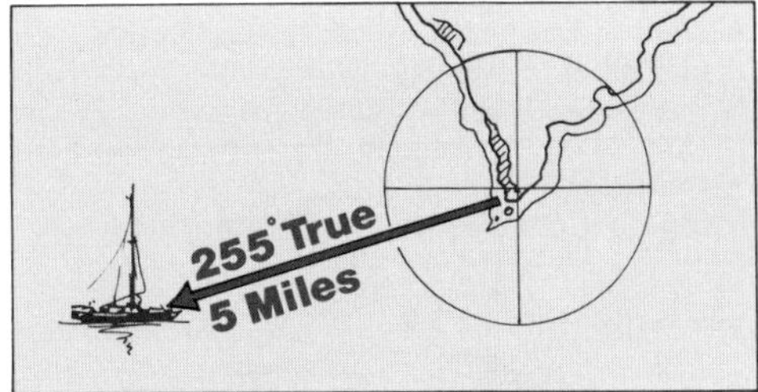

POSITIONS MUST BE GIVEN IN LAT. LONG. OR TRUE BEARINGS FROM A WELL DEFINED CHARTED POSITION WITH DISTANCE OFF. (e.g. Position 255° from South Head, 5 miles.)

If it is onboard, an Emergency Position Indicating Radio Beacon (EPIRB) should be activated to raise the alarm and help the rescue services home in on you.

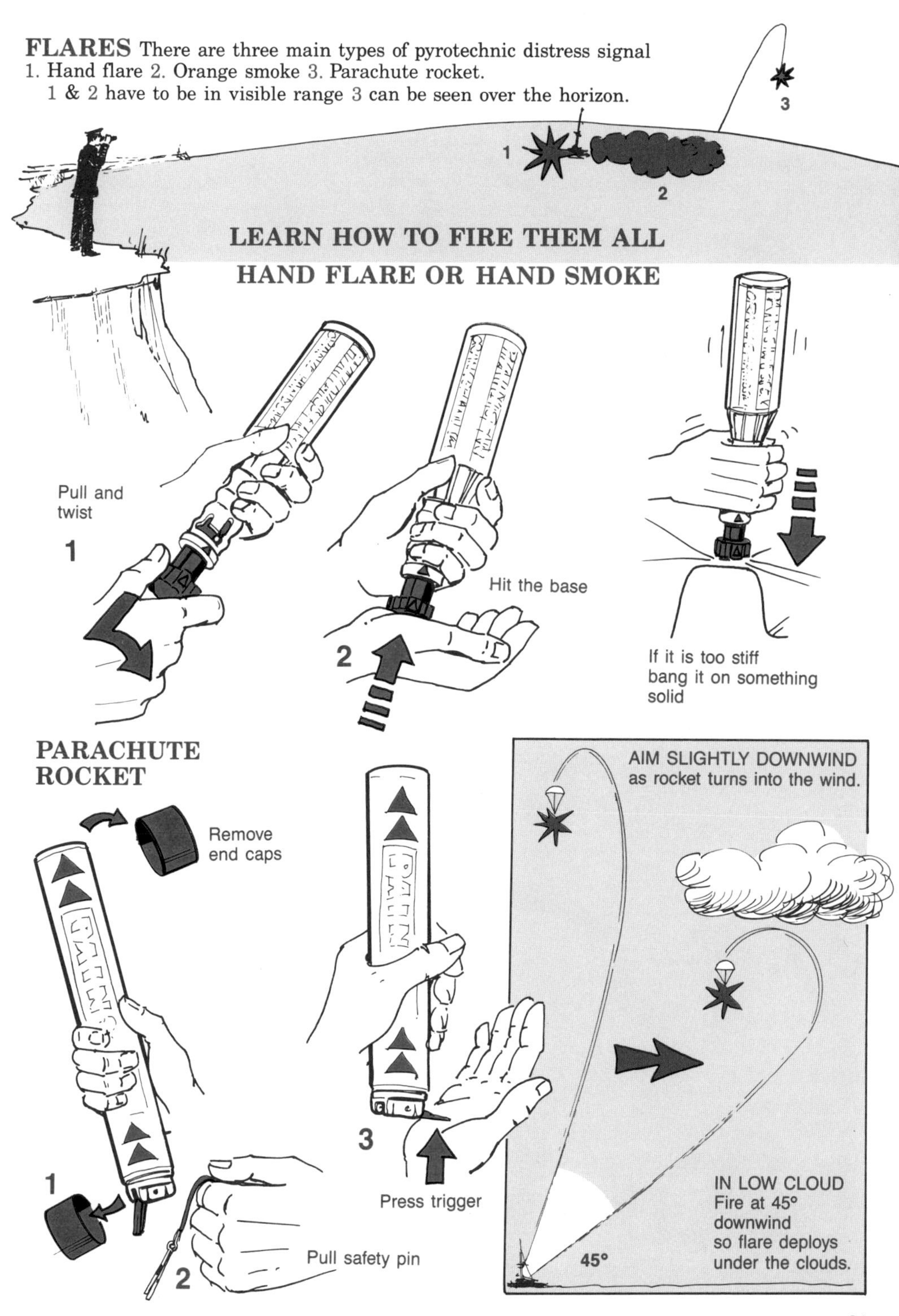
FLARES There are three main types of pyrotechnic distress signal
1. Hand flare 2. Orange smoke 3. Parachute rocket.
1 & 2 have to be in visible range 3 can be seen over the horizon.
1
2
3
LEARN HOW TO FIRE THEM ALL
HAND FLARE OR HAND SMOKE
Pull and twist
1
Hit the base
2
If it is too stiff bang it on something solid
PARACHUTE ROCKET
Remove end caps
1
2
Pull safety pin
3
Press trigger
AIM SLIGHTLY DOWNWIND as rocket turns into the wind.
IN LOW CLOUD Fire at 45° downwind so flare deploys under the clouds.
45°

KNOTS

BOWLINE

The bowline is the best knot for forming an eye or loop, it doesn't jam and can be undone easily.

It can be tied in several ways and many people still think of it as *'the rabbit comes out of his hole, round the tree, and back down the hole again'*.
On slippery rope an extra half hitch adds security.

It can also be tied by twisting ....

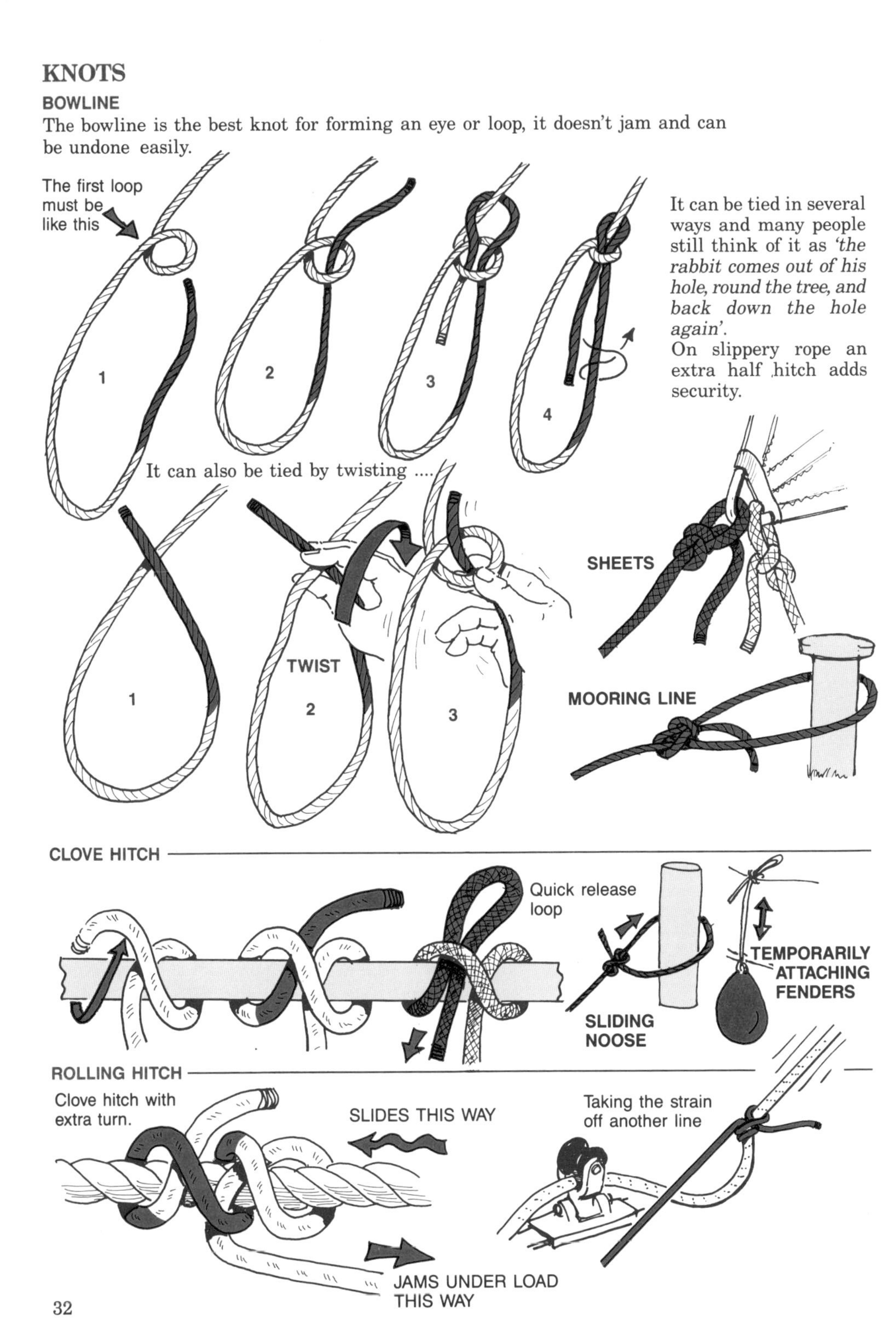

ROUND TURN AND TWO HALF HITCHES

Very secure and can be let go under tension.

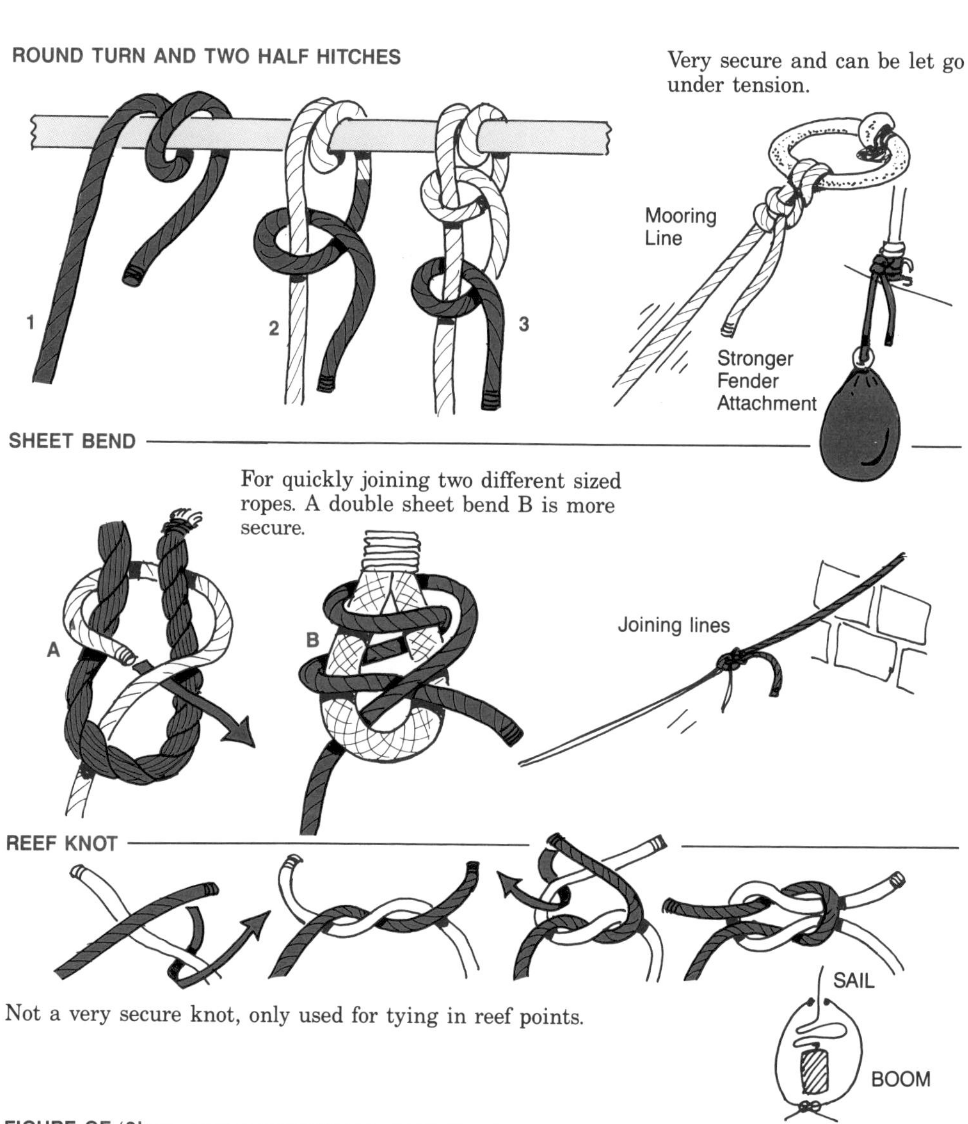

SHEET BEND

For quickly joining two different sized ropes. A double sheet bend B is more secure.

REEF KNOT

Not a very secure knot, only used for tying in reef points.

FIGURE OF '8'

Used as a 'stopper' knot so the line doesn't escape through a fitting. Doesn't jam and can be undone easily.

The best way to learn knots is to get someone to show you – then practise, practise, practise!

LINES UNDER LOAD

The sailor like the cowboy can control quite high loads by TAKING A TURN AROUND SOMETHING.
The sailor's equivalent to a saddle horn is called A CLEAT. They come in many shapes and sizes but all do the same job.

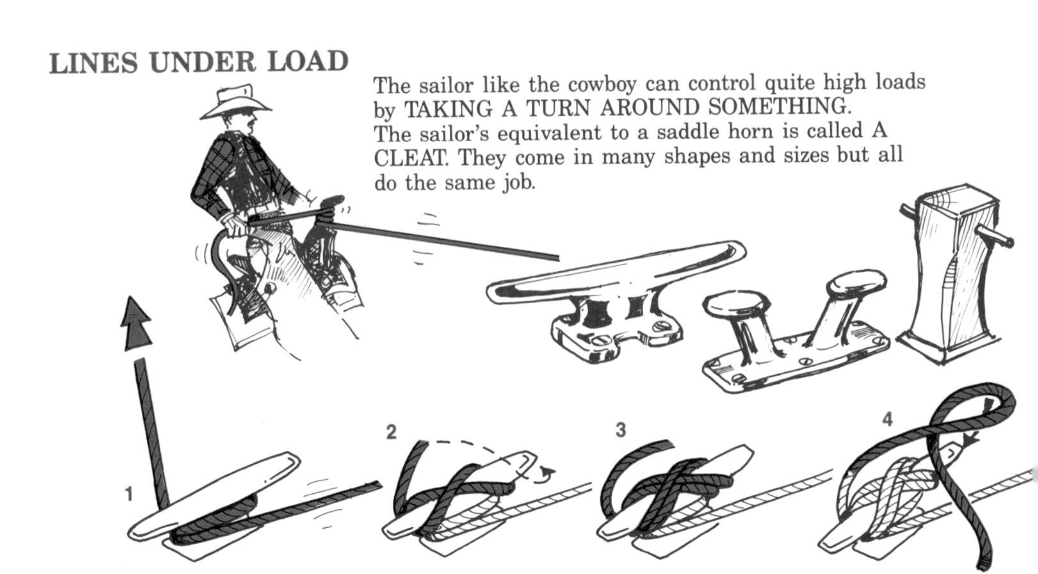

1. To control the line take a turn around the *back* of the cleat and pull.
2. To secure the line, start wrapping *'figure of eight'* turns around the cleat.
3. Several turns produce enough friction to hold the line.
4. A 'twisted' locking turn can be added for extra security but should not be used on sheets, which might have to be released quickly.

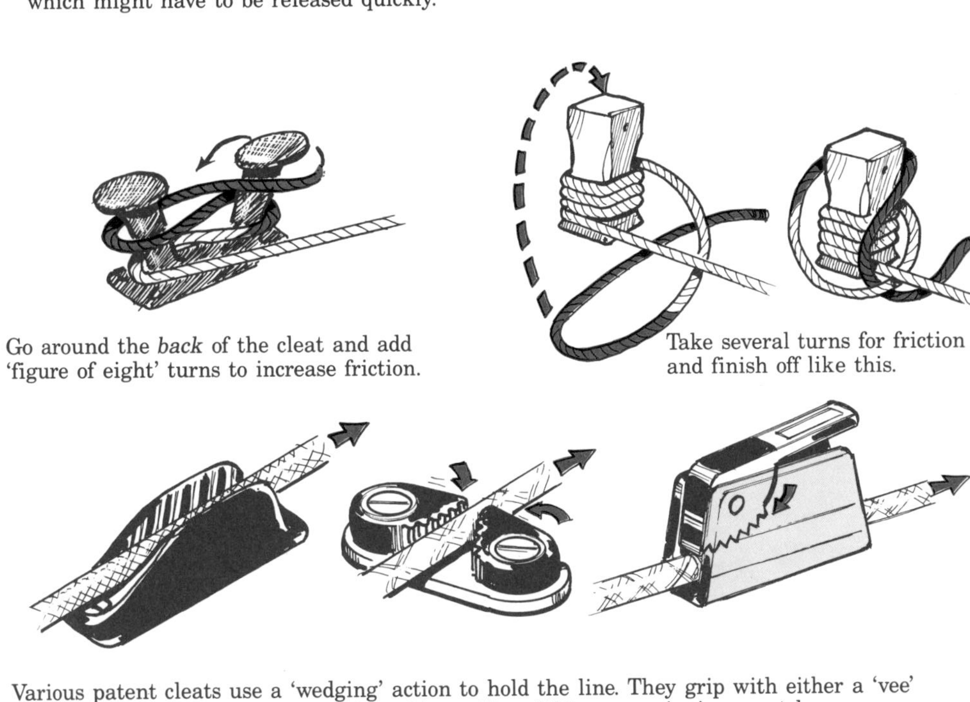

Go around the *back* of the cleat and add 'figure of eight' turns to increase friction.

Take several turns for friction and finish off like this.

Various patent cleats use a 'wedging' action to hold the line. They grip with either a 'vee' notch or clamping jaws and are released by pulling, lifting or springing a catch.

COILS

A regular rhythm of say an arm's width creates an even coil.

Laid rope needs to be coiled *clockwise* and given a *right hand* twist in each turn. Then stowed like this.

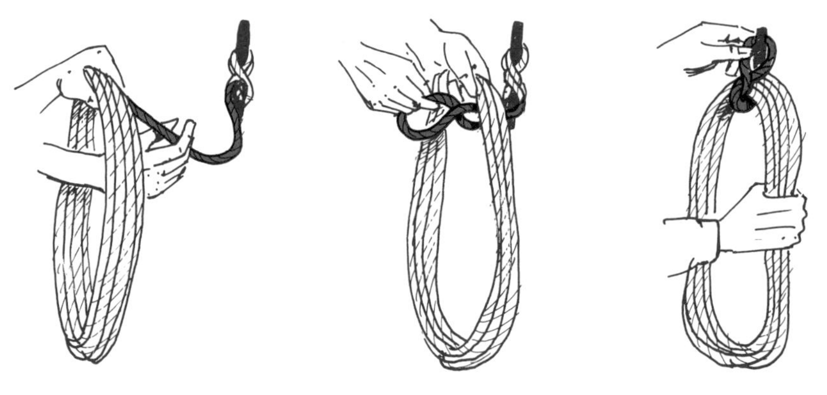

A halyard can be stowed on a mast cleat like this. Although some plaited lines tend to form 'figure of eight' coils rather than neat circles.

THROWING A LINE

Coil the line as above and divide it in two. Swing and throw one coil underhand while releasing the other coil as you do so.

COMING ALONGSIDE

Once lines and fenders are prepared the shore crew should stand by the shrouds with a coiled mooring line in one hand. Hold on with the other hand and step over the guardrail and stand outboard. Don't be too eager to leap ashore, as the skipper might decide to go around again if he's not happy with his first approach.

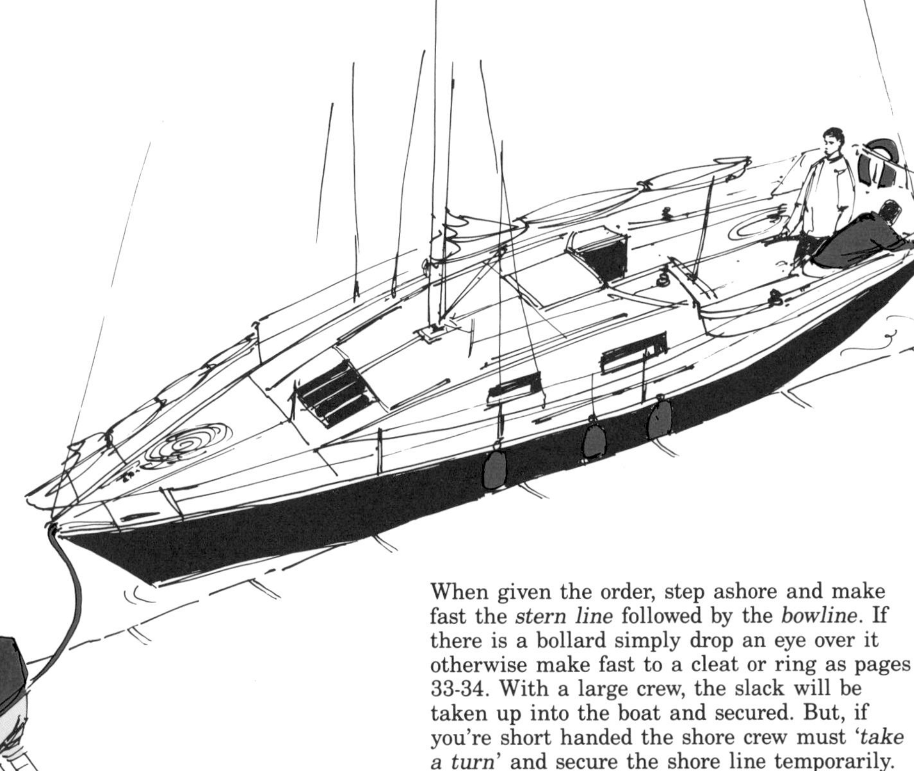

When given the order, step ashore and make fast the *stern line* followed by the *bowline*. If there is a bollard simply drop an eye over it otherwise make fast to a cleat or ring as pages 33-34. With a large crew, the slack will be taken up into the boat and secured. But, if you're short handed the shore crew must '*take a turn*' and secure the shore line temporarily.

If you are mooring to a short pontoon it might be necessary to rig the stern line through a genoa fairlead like this. By quickly 'taking a turn' this line can also be used as a brake if there is a tail wind.

Try not to obstruct the skipper's view at this critical moment.

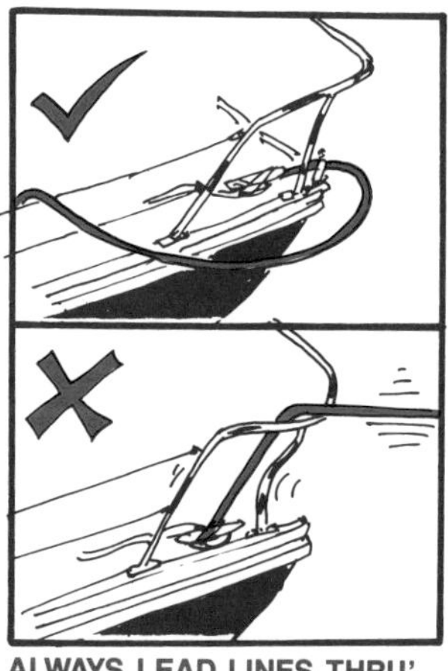

ALWAYS LEAD LINES THRU' FAIRLEADS & *UNDER* RAILS

The skipper will tell you which side to rig fenders and lines (see pages 32-33) and what you'll be mooring to Fenders high for '*boat to boat*'' fenders low for "*boat to pontoon*". But always arrange them around the widest part of the boat, and tie them on *before* you put them over the side. They can then be adjusted for height.
In strong winds, when the noise can drown spoken orders, always LOOK at the skipper for the signal to step ashore.

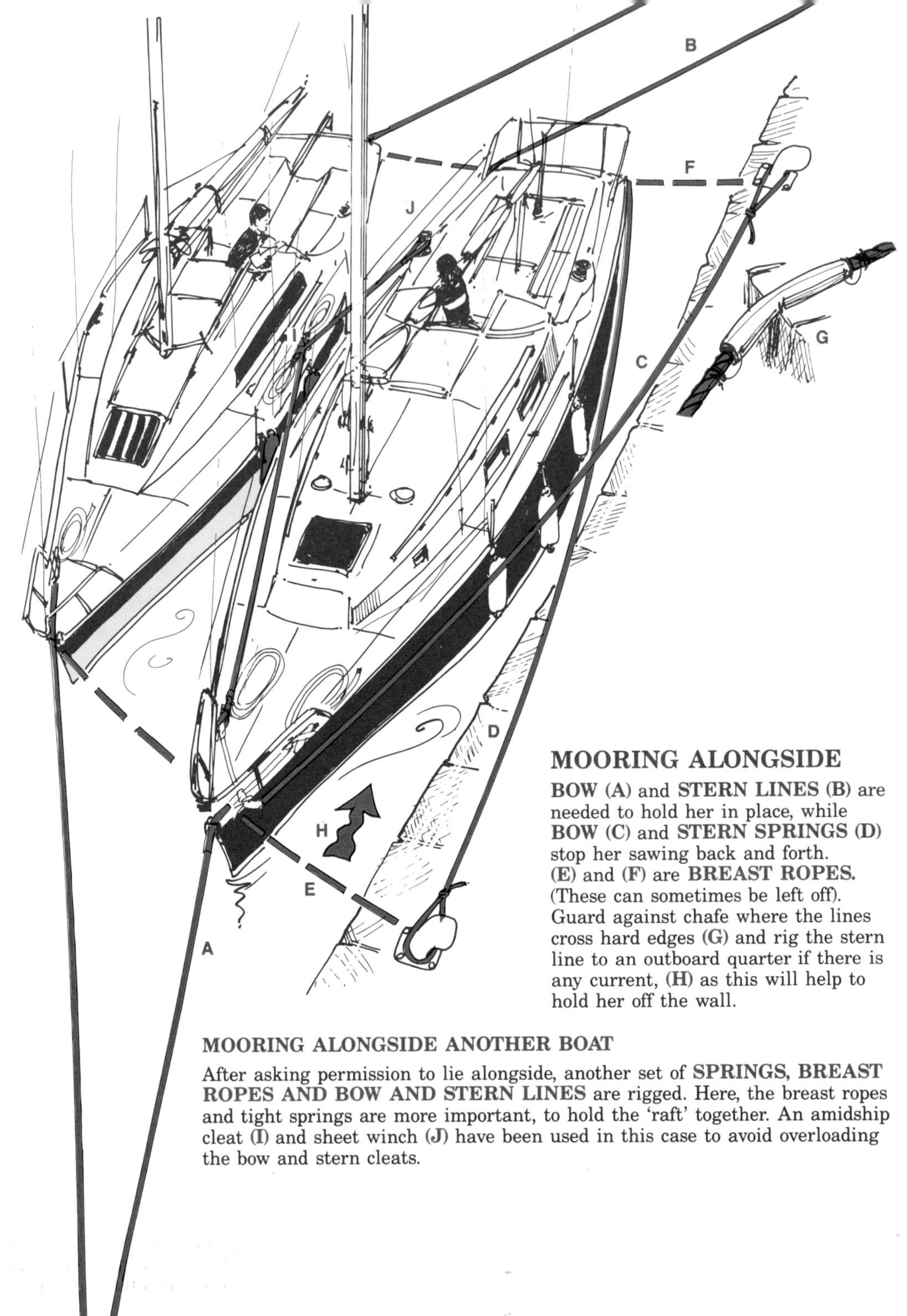

MOORING ALONGSIDE

BOW (A) and **STERN LINES (B)** are needed to hold her in place, while **BOW (C)** and **STERN SPRINGS (D)** stop her sawing back and forth. **(E)** and **(F)** are **BREAST ROPES.** (These can sometimes be left off). Guard against chafe where the lines cross hard edges **(G)** and rig the stern line to an outboard quarter if there is any current, **(H)** as this will help to hold her off the wall.

MOORING ALONGSIDE ANOTHER BOAT

After asking permission to lie alongside, another set of **SPRINGS, BREAST ROPES AND BOW AND STERN LINES** are rigged. Here, the breast ropes and tight springs are more important, to hold the 'raft' together. An amidship cleat **(I)** and sheet winch **(J)** have been used in this case to avoid overloading the bow and stern cleats.

MAKING FAST ALONGSIDE

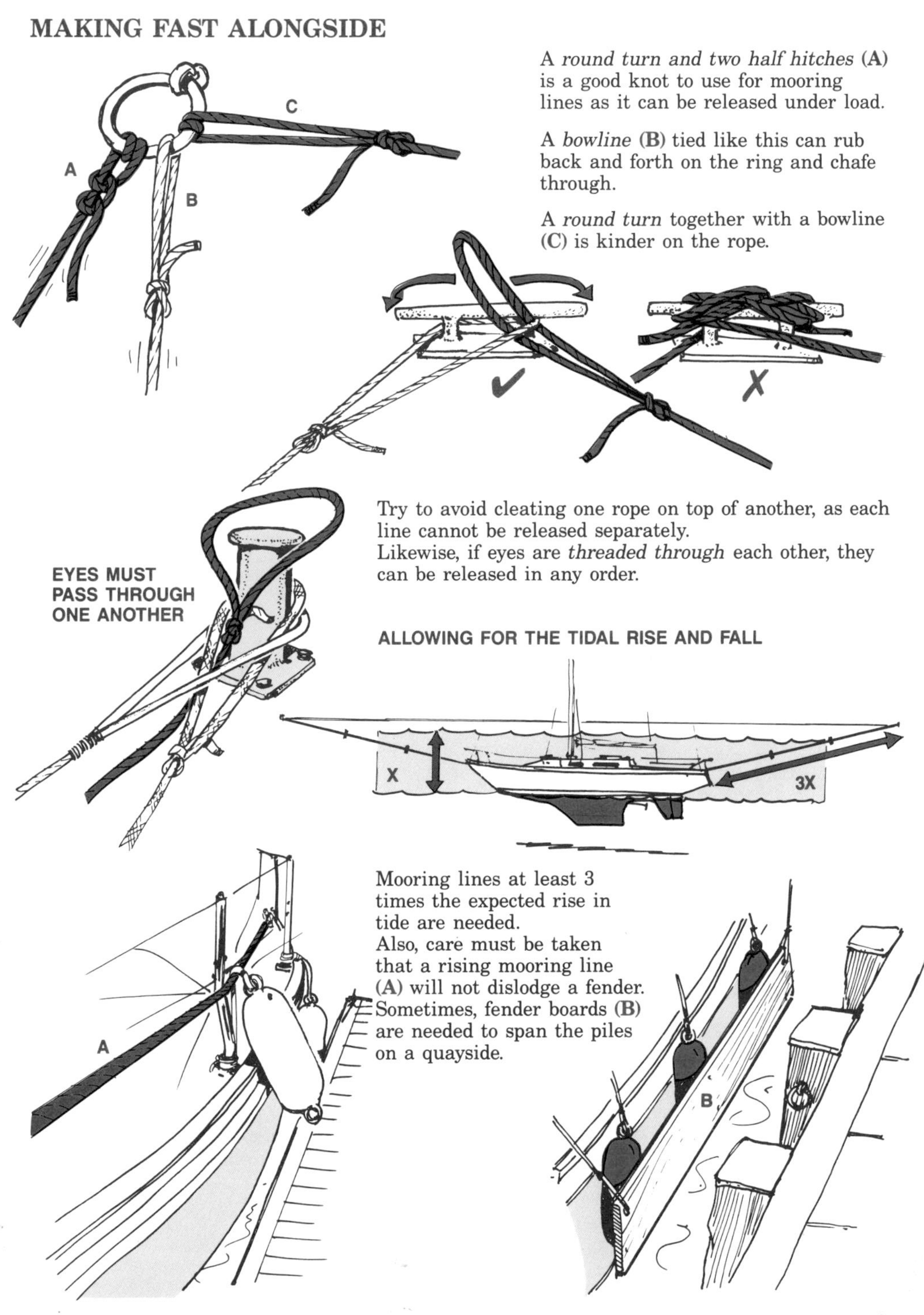

A *round turn and two half hitches* (**A**) is a good knot to use for mooring lines as it can be released under load.

A *bowline* (**B**) tied like this can rub back and forth on the ring and chafe through.

A *round turn* together with a bowline (**C**) is kinder on the rope.

Try to avoid cleating one rope on top of another, as each line cannot be released separately.
Likewise, if eyes are *threaded through* each other, they can be released in any order.

ALLOWING FOR THE TIDAL RISE AND FALL

Mooring lines at least 3 times the expected rise in tide are needed.
Also, care must be taken that a rising mooring line (**A**) will not dislodge a fender.
Sometimes, fender boards (**B**) are needed to span the piles on a quayside.

LEAVING AN ALONGSIDE MOORING

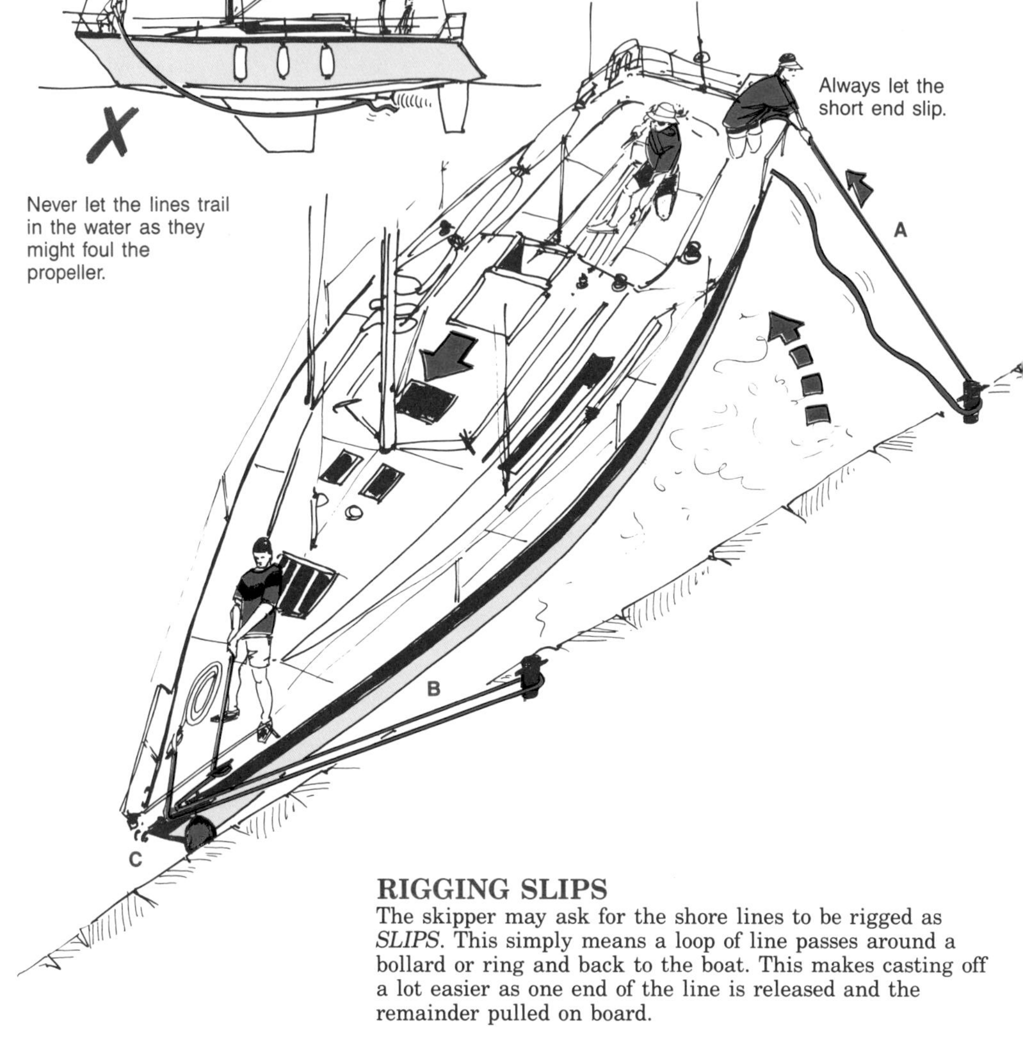

RIGGING SLIPS

The skipper may ask for the shore lines to be rigged as *SLIPS*. This simply means a loop of line passes around a bollard or ring and back to the boat. This makes casting off a lot easier as one end of the line is released and the remainder pulled on board.

(A) When there will be no load on the slip it can be rigged from the cleat, round the bollard and back to the crew's hand *above the rail. But,* the skipper may want to power againt the slip to push the boat out. In that case the line must come back onboard through a fairlead and a turn be taken around a cleat **(B)**. Also, an extra fender **(C)** needs to be placed at the bow or stern to cushion the turning boat.

LEAVING A RAFT

Normally, a boat will leave an inside berth in a raft *down tide* so the current will push the boats together again. An extra long line **(A)** is rigged behind her and outside of everything to help pull the pack together again. All her mooring lines and shorelines are cast off leaving her breast ropes made up as slips. Once she's clear **(A)** is tensioned up and all the shorelines re-rigged.

THINGS TO WATCH OUT FOR

Usually there are *many willing helpers* to ease the boat out. But, this can be a mixed blessing as their concentrated weight on one side can heel the boat and foul the rigging **(A)**. Also, make sure the extra line does not foul the danbuoy **(B)** or stowed outboard **(C)** and be sure *all* your lines have been released **(D)**. Fenders also have the nasty habit of becoming entangled at awkward moments!

MOORING BUOYS

Mooring buoys usually have a ring (**A**) to make fast to or some form of *'pick-up buoy'*. The pick-up buoy can either be attached to the chain strop on the large buoy (**B**) or to a ground chain (**C**) with an eye in it.

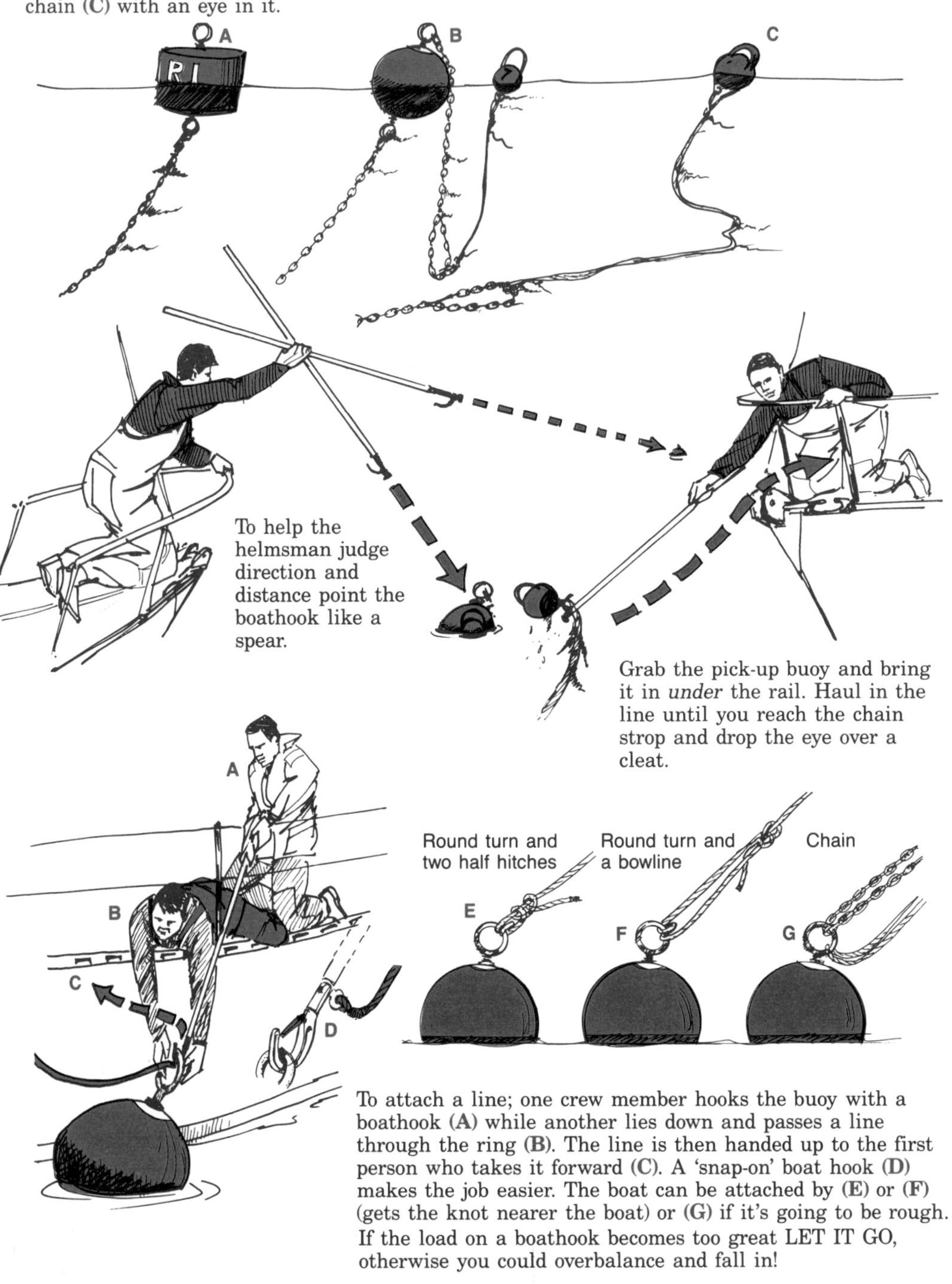

To help the helmsman judge direction and distance point the boathook like a spear.

Grab the pick-up buoy and bring it in *under* the rail. Haul in the line until you reach the chain strop and drop the eye over a cleat.

To attach a line; one crew member hooks the buoy with a boathook (**A**) while another lies down and passes a line through the ring (**B**). The line is then handed up to the first person who takes it forward (**C**). A 'snap-on' boat hook (**D**) makes the job easier. The boat can be attached by (**E**) or (**F**) (gets the knot nearer the boat) or (**G**) if it's going to be rough. If the load on a boathook becomes too great LET IT GO, otherwise you could overbalance and fall in!

ANCHORING

A. Understand how the length of chain is marked, so the correct amount can be flaked down on deck.

B. Flaking down lets the chain run out freely.

C. Secure the cleat so you can always let out more line.

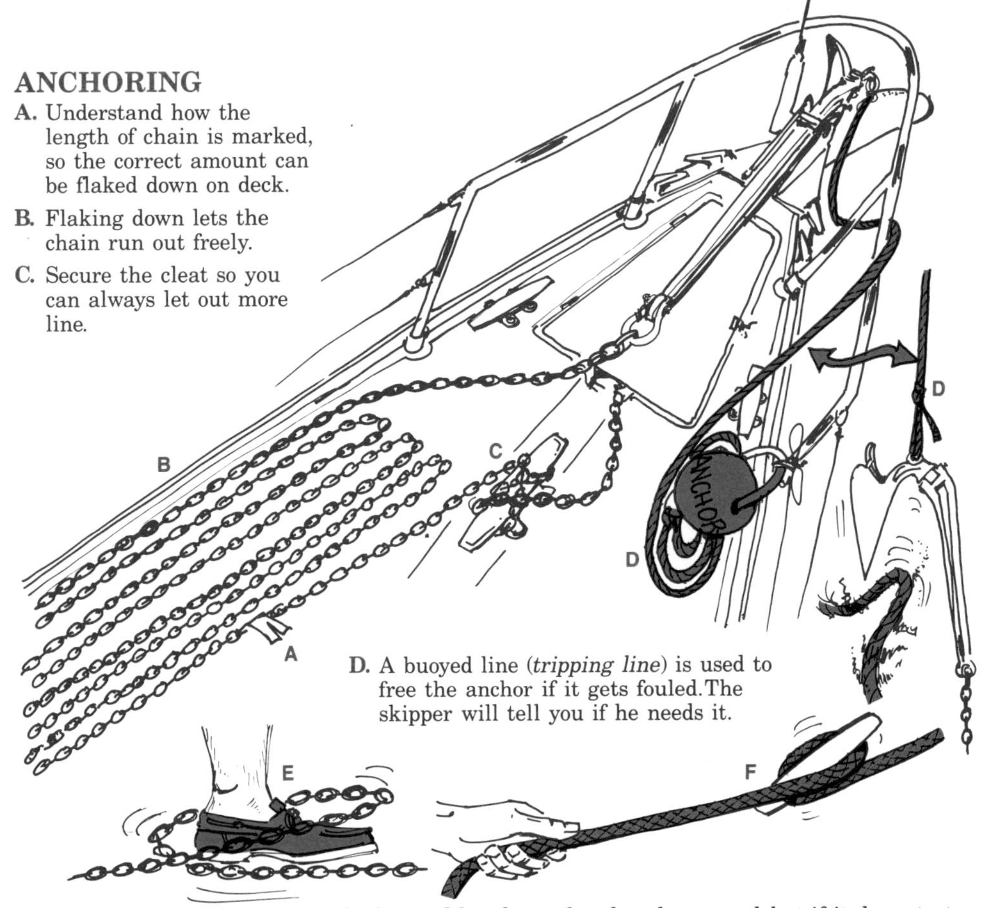

D. A buoyed line (*tripping line*) is used to free the anchor if it gets fouled. The skipper will tell you if he needs it.

The anchor chain (cable) should be lowered hand over hand under control *but* if it does start snaking out **(E)** STAND WELL CLEAR! If asked to 'SNUB' the cable by taking a turn – KEEP YOUR HANDS WELL BACK FROM THE CLEAT **(F)**.

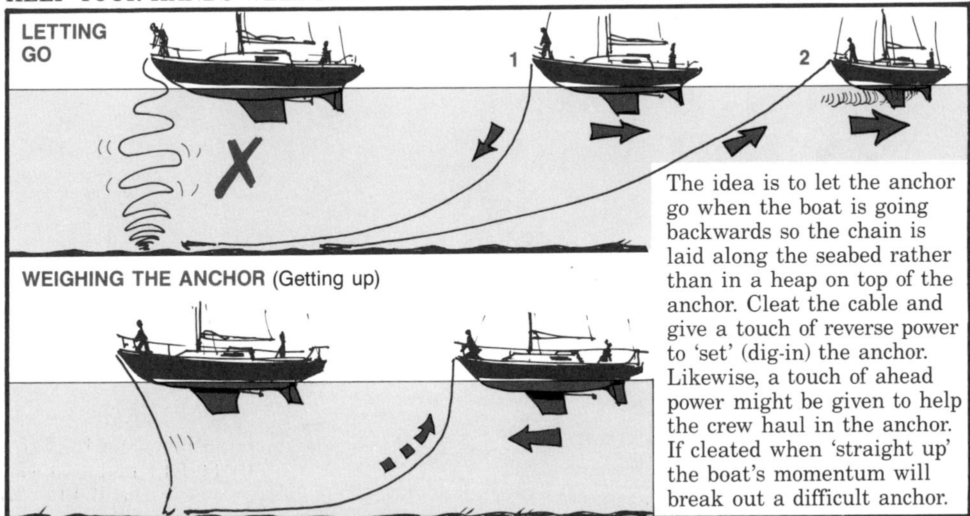

The idea is to let the anchor go when the boat is going backwards so the chain is laid along the seabed rather than in a heap on top of the anchor. Cleat the cable and give a touch of reverse power to 'set' (dig-in) the anchor. Likewise, a touch of ahead power might be given to help the crew haul in the anchor. If cleated when 'straight up' the boat's momentum will break out a difficult anchor.

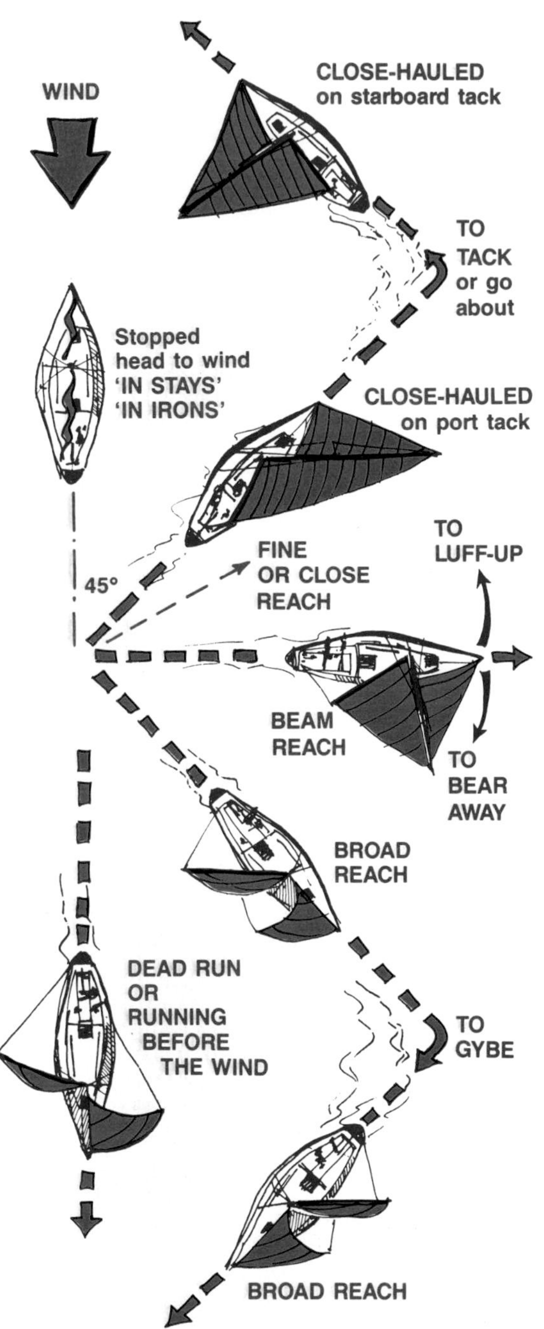

POINTS OF SAIL AND SAILING TERMS

CLOSE HAULED is as close to the wind as the boat will sail (say about 45°)

To sail towards the wind a boat must **TACK** or zig-zag. (Also known as beating.)

STARBOARD TACK is when the wind comes over the starboard side.

PORT TACK is when the wind comes over the port side.

TO TACK OR GO ABOUT is to change from one tack to the other by putting the bow through the wind.

FINE OR CLOSE REACH is a course between close-hauled and a beam reach.

TO LUFF-UP is to steer the boat towards the wind.

TO BEAR AWAY is to steer away from the wind.

BEAM REACH is when the wind comes over the beam (ie. 90°).

TO GYBE is to let the mainsail change sides by putting the stern through the wind.

BROAD REACH is when the wind comes over the quarter.

DEAD RUN OR RUNNING BEFORE THE WIND is when the wind is blowing over the stern.

LOOK UP

WATCH THE WIND INDICATOR!

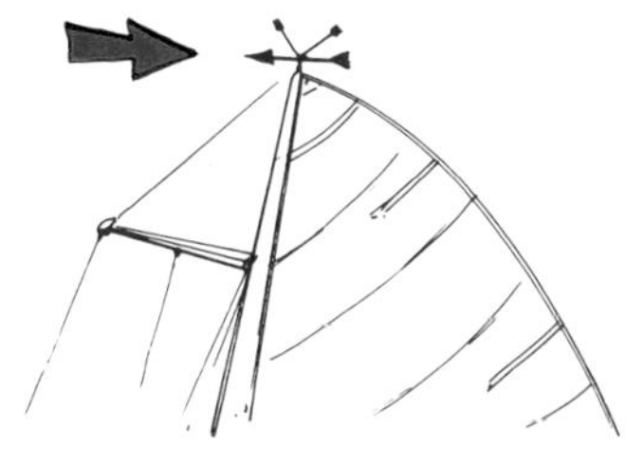

SAILS

Headsails can be attached to the stay by a grooved foil (**A**) or clipped on with hanks (**B**).

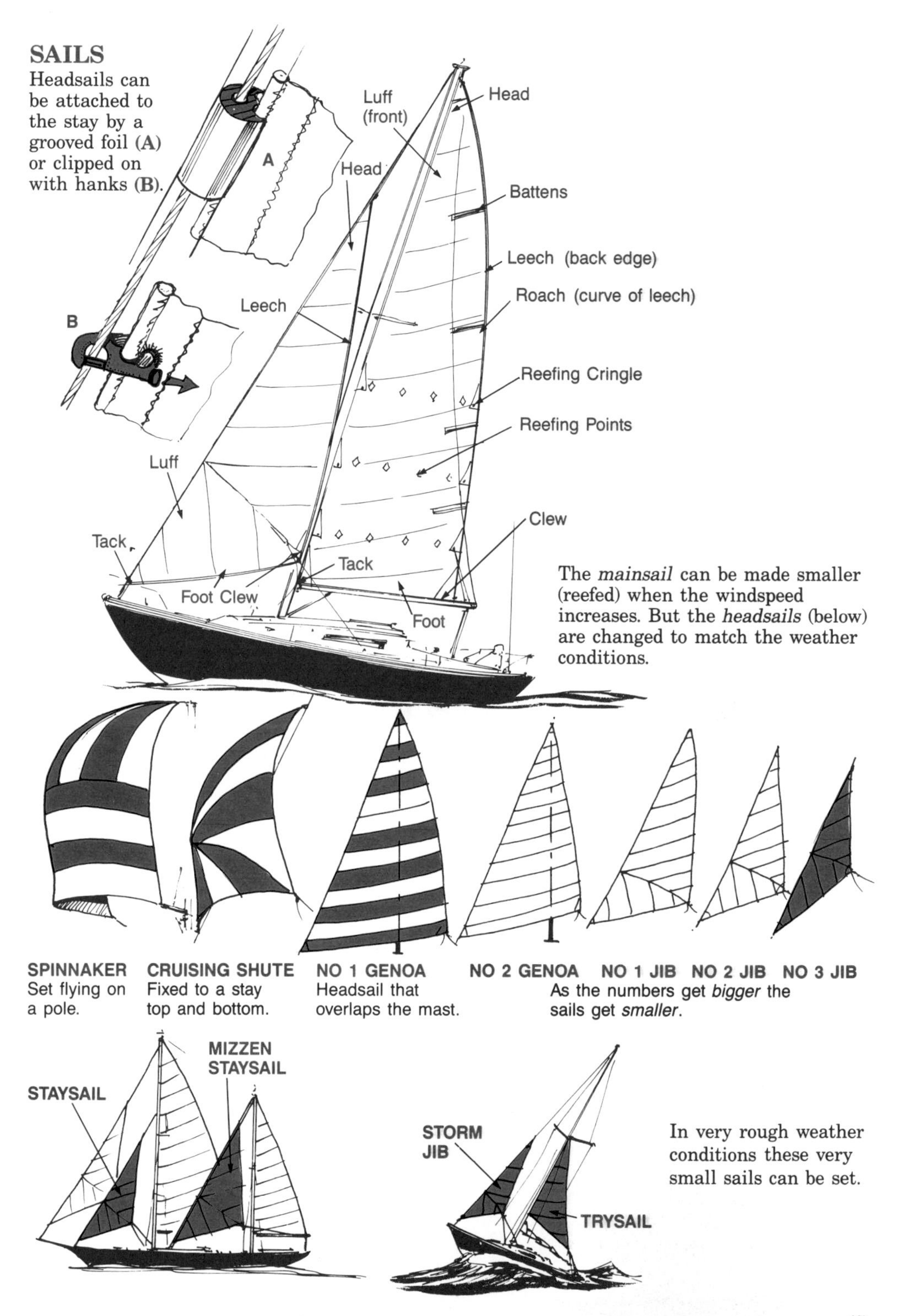

The *mainsail* can be made smaller (reefed) when the windspeed increases. But the *headsails* (below) are changed to match the weather conditions.

In very rough weather conditions these very small sails can be set.

STOWING SAILS

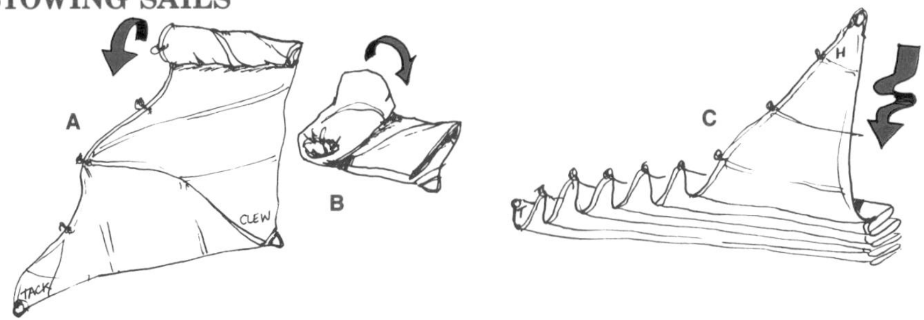

Small headsails can be rolled (**A**) from *head* to *tack* and then (**B**) *tack* to *clew*, this minimises creases. Larger sails (**C**) can be flaked down, but this is usually only possible in harbour.

STOWING AT SEA

Sails can be folded at sea but most people simply stuff them into a sailbag.

1. Secure the bag so it doesn't blow away.

2. Remove the sheets and halyard and secure them.

3. Leave the sail hanked to the stay and start stuffing the sail into the bag *clew first*.

4. Unhank the sail starting at the *head*.

5. Make sure the *tack* is near the opening of the bag as this is the first corner to be rigged when *bending on* a sail. Some people pass the draw string through the tack to make identification easier at night.

BENDING ON SAILS

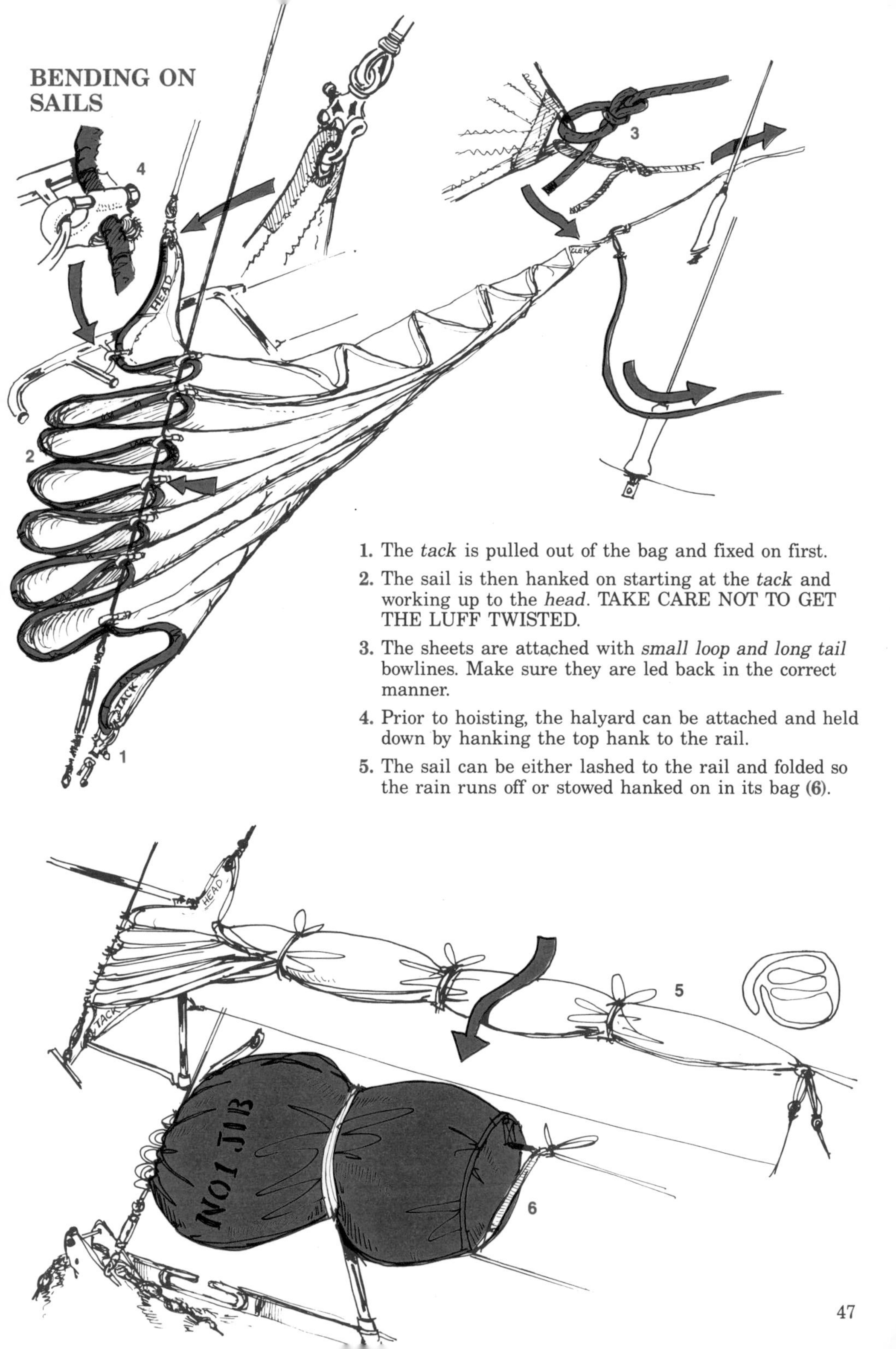

1. The *tack* is pulled out of the bag and fixed on first.
2. The sail is then hanked on starting at the *tack* and working up to the *head*. TAKE CARE NOT TO GET THE LUFF TWISTED.
3. The sheets are attached with *small loop and long tail* bowlines. Make sure they are led back in the correct manner.
4. Prior to hoisting, the halyard can be attached and held down by hanking the top hank to the rail.
5. The sail can be either lashed to the rail and folded so the rain runs off or stowed hanked on in its bag (**6**).

HOISTING

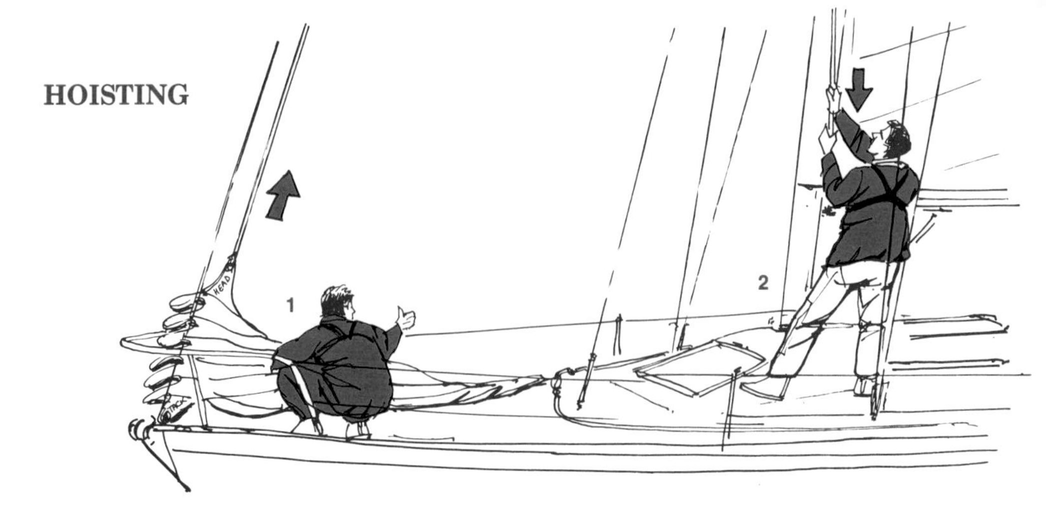

1. The bow man checks the *hanks, sheets* and *halyard*, gets to *weather* and signals it's OK to hoist.
2. The crew on the halyard LOOKS UP (**A**) and checks the halyard is not twisted around the forestay or fouling the spreaders (**B**).
3. If it is clear, the halyard is hauled in smartly either by pulling directly or by taking a turn around the halyard winch (**C**).

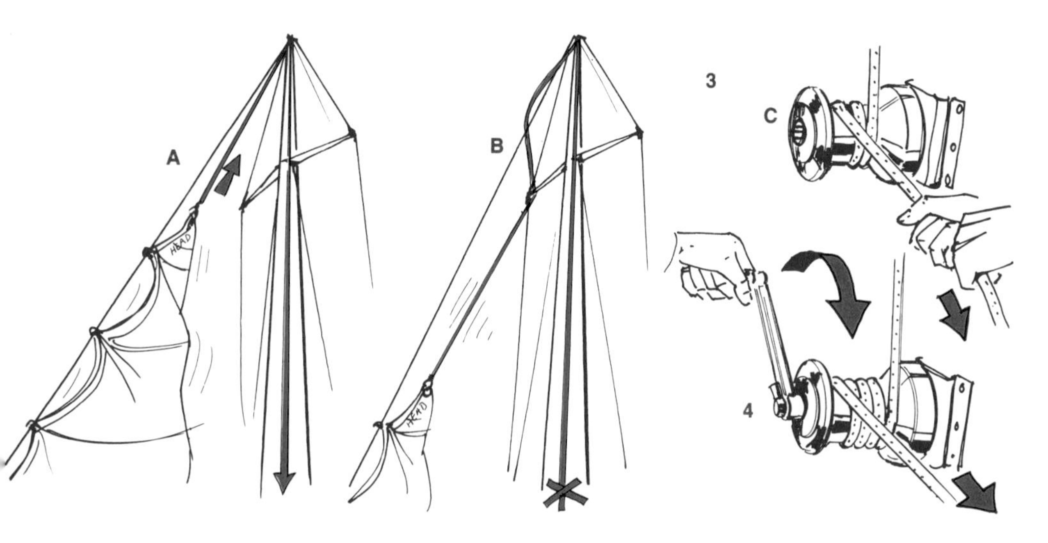

4. Take several turns around the winch and use the winch handle to tension the luff of the sail. (Luff tension is right when horizontal luff creases disappear but vertical creases are not formed when the sail is sheeted in.) Coil and cleat the halyard (see page 35).

CHANGING HEADSAILS

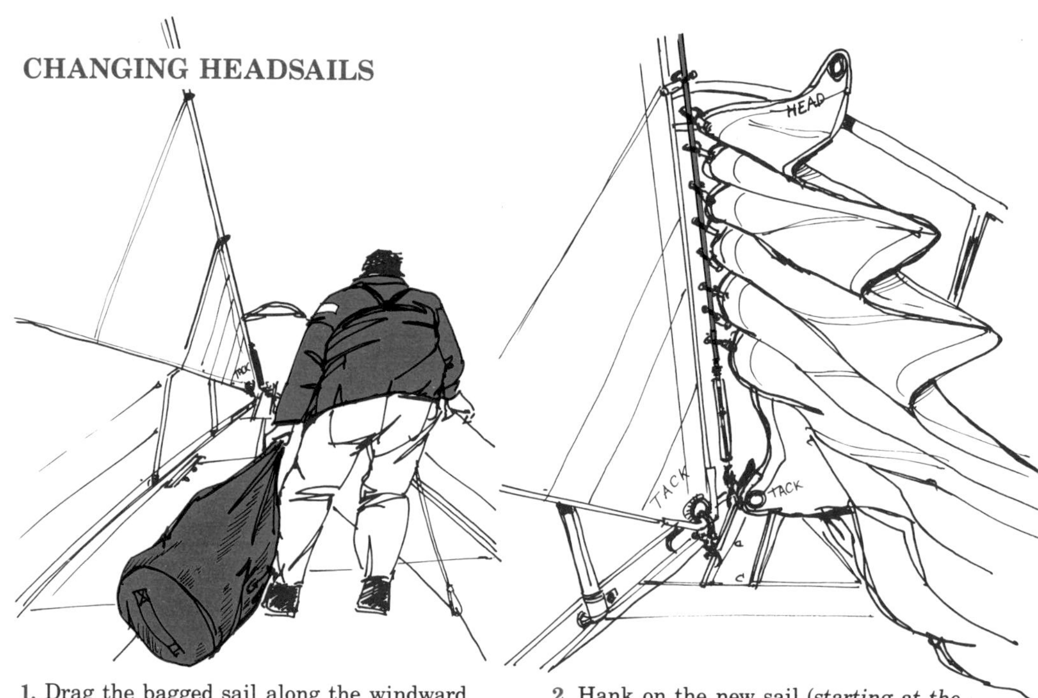

1. Drag the bagged sail along the windward sidedeck and make sure you are hooked on in heavy weather.

2. Hank on the new sail (*starting at the tack*) below the first hank of the old sail. Secure the bag.

3. Tension is kept on the halyard by letting it slip around the winch as the sail is pulled down.

4. Pull on the luff of the old sail to lower it. Remove the halyard and secure it. Transfer the sheets to the new sail.

5. Bag or stow the old sail and unhank. Transfer the halyard to the new sail and hoist when ready.

HEADFOILS

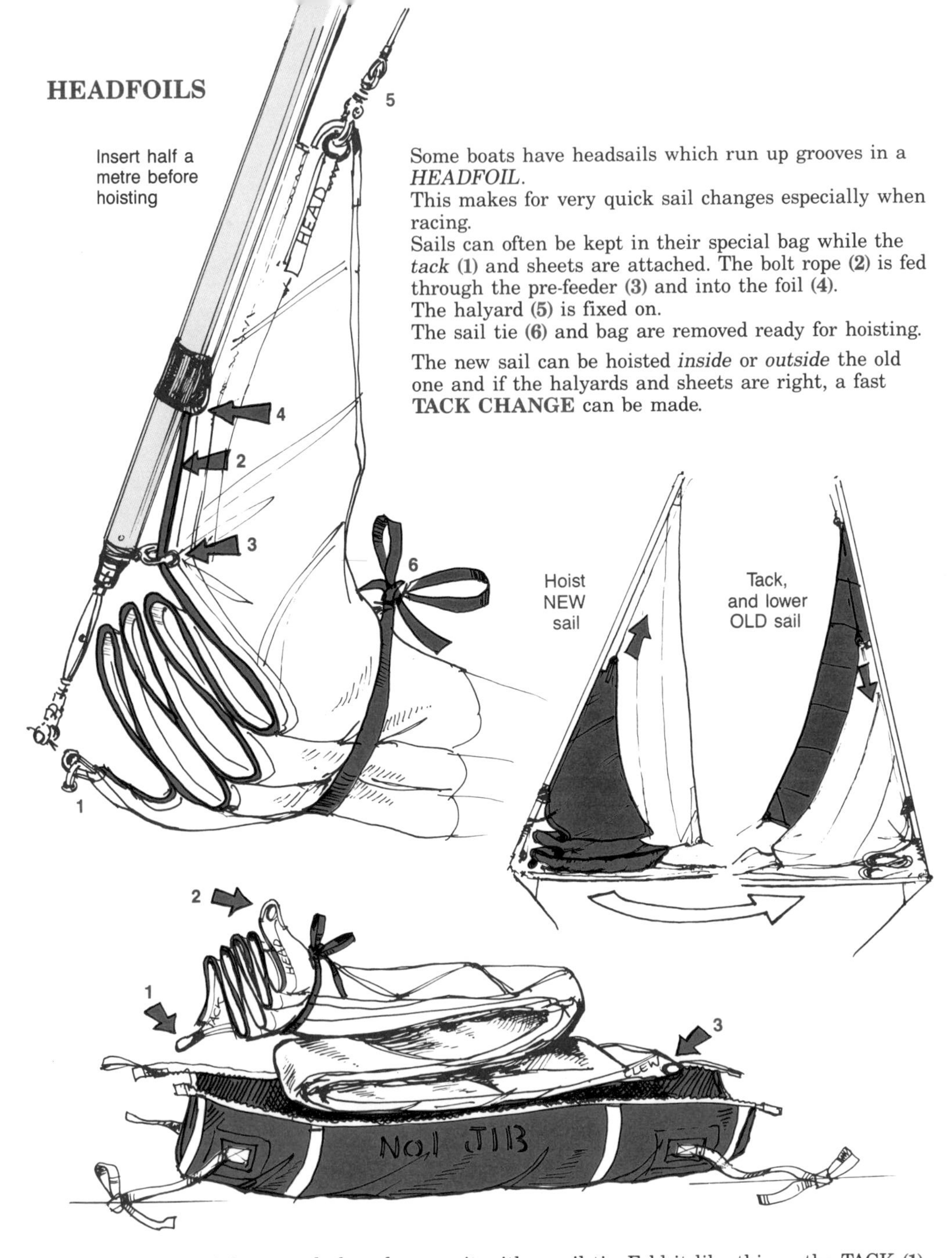

Some boats have headsails which run up grooves in a *HEADFOIL*.
This makes for very quick sail changes especially when racing.
Sails can often be kept in their special bag while the *tack* **(1)** and sheets are attached. The bolt rope **(2)** is fed through the pre-feeder **(3)** and into the foil **(4)**.
The halyard **(5)** is fixed on.
The sail tie **(6)** and bag are removed ready for hoisting.

The new sail can be hoisted *inside* or *outside* the old one and if the halyards and sheets are right, a fast **TACK CHANGE** can be made.

Flake the old sail down on deck and secure it with a sail tie. Fold it like this so the TACK (1), HEAD (2) and CLEW (3) are readily accessible in the bag. Bags vary in design, but usually have a full length zip which can sometimes just be pulled apart. ALWAYS TIE THE BAG TO THE BOAT.

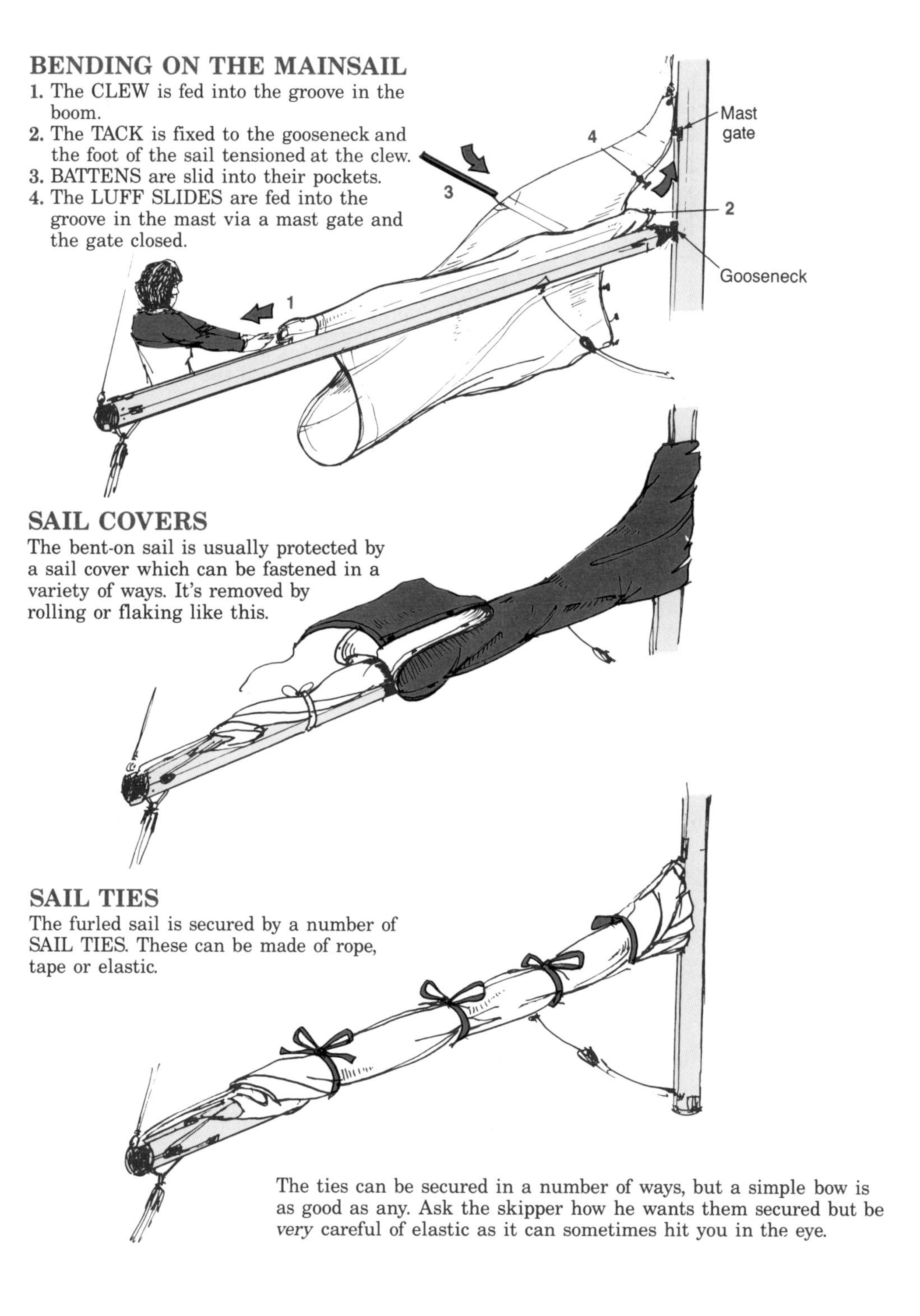

BENDING ON THE MAINSAIL

1. The CLEW is fed into the groove in the boom.
2. The TACK is fixed to the gooseneck and the foot of the sail tensioned at the clew.
3. BATTENS are slid into their pockets.
4. The LUFF SLIDES are fed into the groove in the mast via a mast gate and the gate closed.

SAIL COVERS

The bent-on sail is usually protected by a sail cover which can be fastened in a variety of ways. It's removed by rolling or flaking like this.

SAIL TIES

The furled sail is secured by a number of SAIL TIES. These can be made of rope, tape or elastic.

The ties can be secured in a number of ways, but a simple bow is as good as any. Ask the skipper how he wants them secured but be *very* careful of elastic as it can sometimes hit you in the eye.

HOISTING THE MAINSAIL

1. Check all sail slides are in groove.
2. Remove sail ties, working forward.
3. Attach halyard.
4. Free sheet and kicking strap.

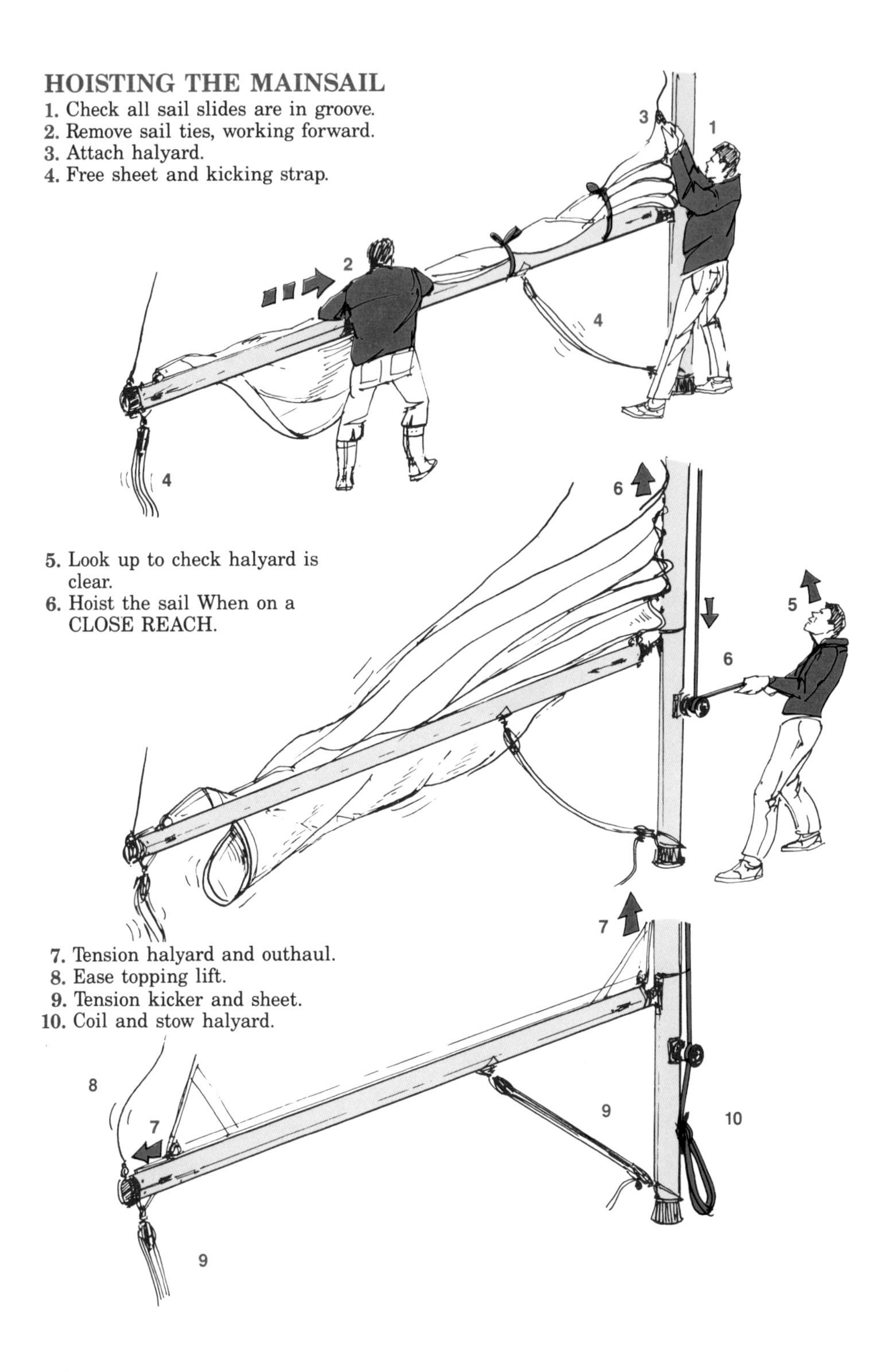

5. Look up to check halyard is clear.
6. Hoist the sail When on a CLOSE REACH.

7. Tension halyard and outhaul.
8. Ease topping lift.
9. Tension kicker and sheet.
10. Coil and stow halyard.

REEFING

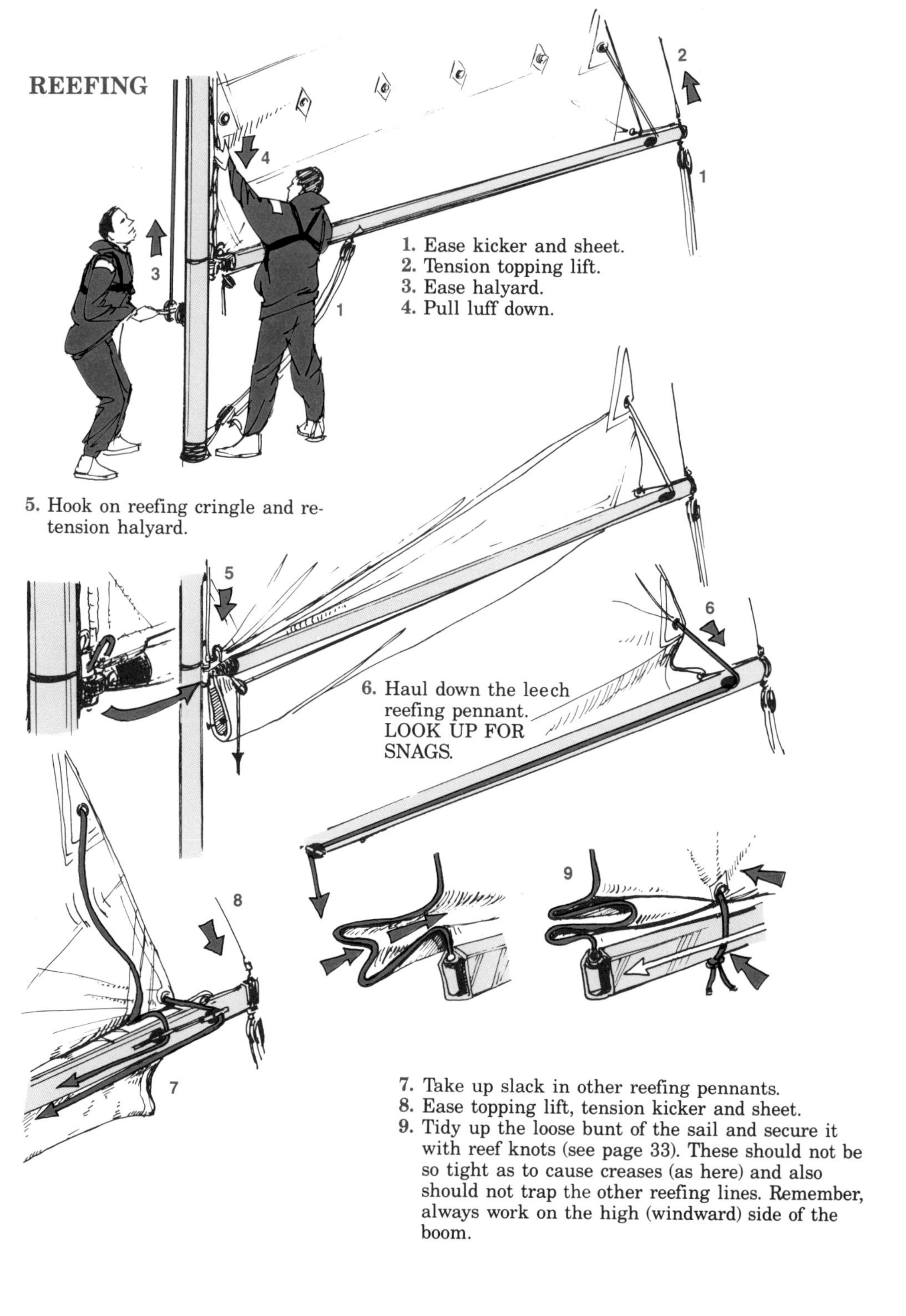

1. Ease kicker and sheet.
2. Tension topping lift.
3. Ease halyard.
4. Pull luff down.

5. Hook on reefing cringle and re-tension halyard.

6. Haul down the leech reefing pennant. LOOK UP FOR SNAGS.

7. Take up slack in other reefing pennants.
8. Ease topping lift, tension kicker and sheet.
9. Tidy up the loose bunt of the sail and secure it with reef knots (see page 33). These should not be so tight as to cause creases (as here) and also should not trap the other reefing lines. Remember, always work on the high (windward) side of the boom.

SHAKING OUT A REEF

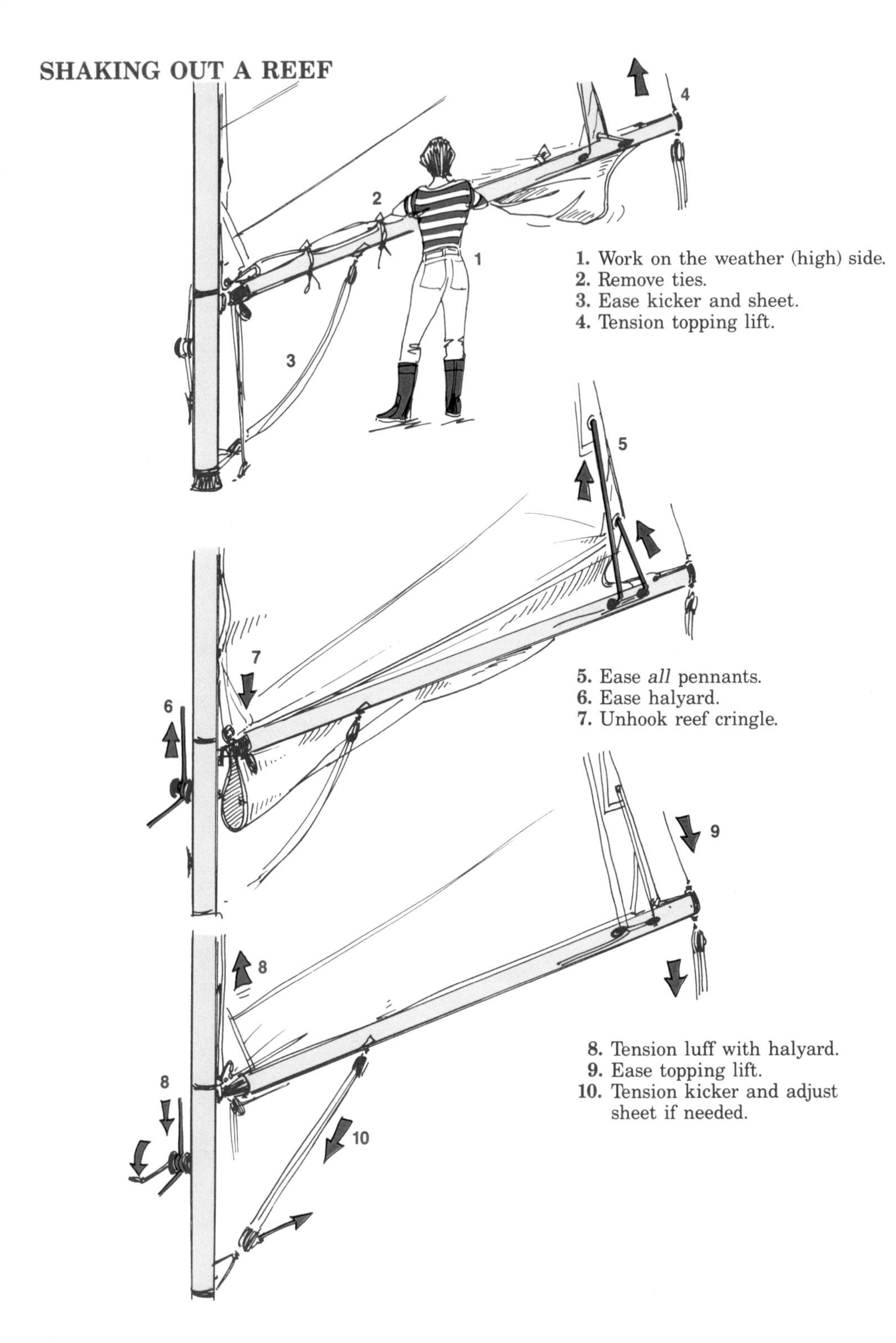

HANDING THE MAINSAIL (Lowering)

1. Ease the main sheet.
2. Ease kicker.
3. Tension topping lift.
4. Ease halyard.
5. Pull luff down.
6. Pull sail aft.
7. When the sail is down tighten the main sheet to steady the boom.
8. Try to flake the sail down or ....

8. .... form a sort of pocket in the sail and push the folds of the sail into it. The top of the pocket can be folded over the sail to act as a cover and let any rain run off.

In heavy weather and short handed add a *safety tuck* to the main sheet (as shown) and haul the sail aft tying it down as you work your way forward.

SAIL CONTROLS

The mainsail is controlled by a powerful block and tackle system called the *mainsheet*. A small force on the mainsheet tail (A) is multiplied by the pulleys to a large force (B).
Subtle sail adjustments can be made by moving the mainsheet across the boat on the *mainsheet track*.
Another smaller set of lines, blocks and cleats (C) are used to control this movement.
The *kicking strap* helps control the shape of the sail and stops the boom lifting when the main sheet is let full out.

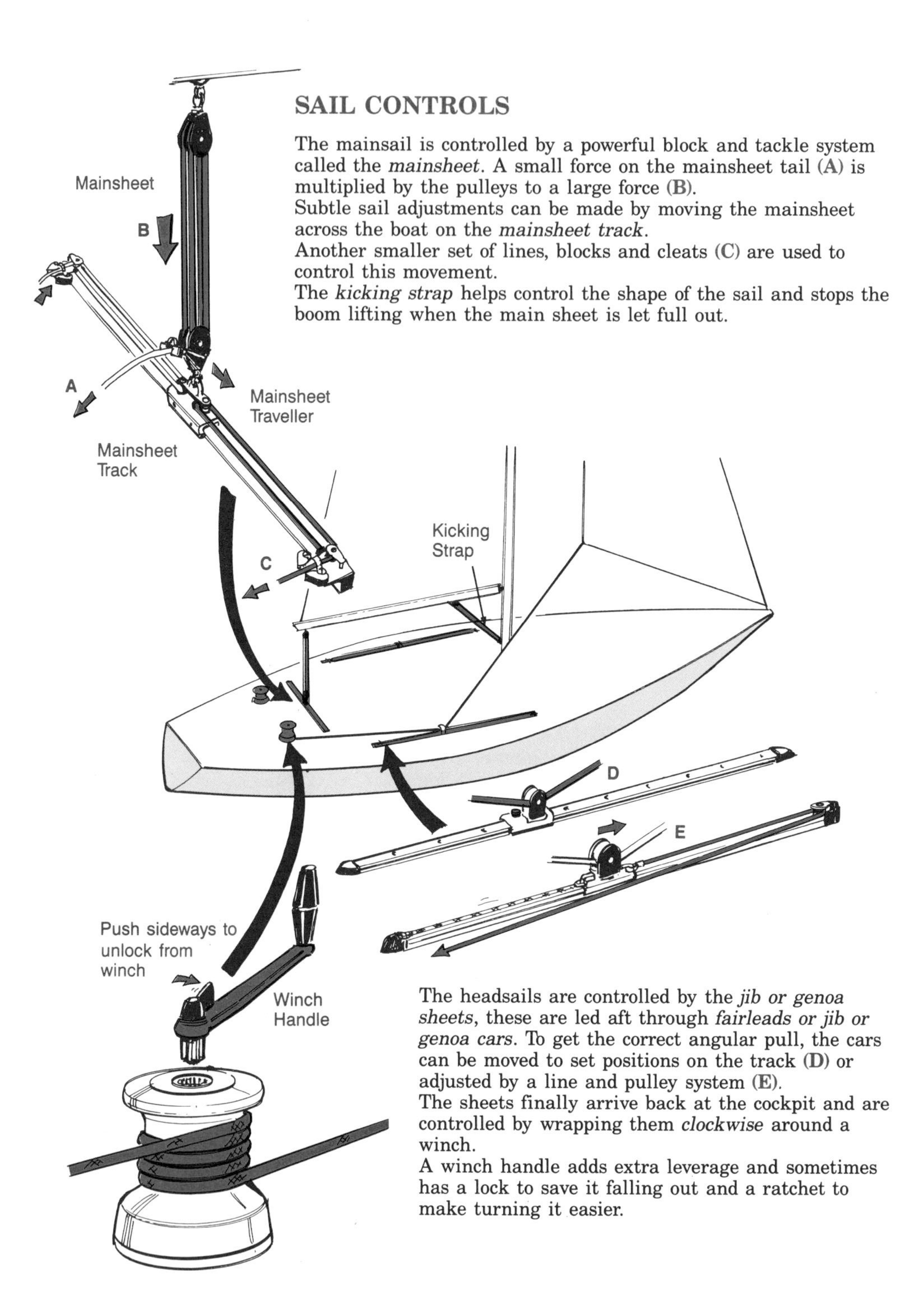

The headsails are controlled by the *jib or genoa sheets*, these are led aft through *fairleads or jib or genoa cars*. To get the correct angular pull, the cars can be moved to set positions on the track (D) or adjusted by a line and pulley system (E).
The sheets finally arrive back at the cockpit and are controlled by wrapping them *clockwise* around a winch.
A winch handle adds extra leverage and sometimes has a lock to save it falling out and a ratchet to make turning it easier.

USING FRICTION

The more turns you make with a rope the more friction you get. So very large forces can be controlled with the minimum of effort. Winches use this principle.

USING WINCHES

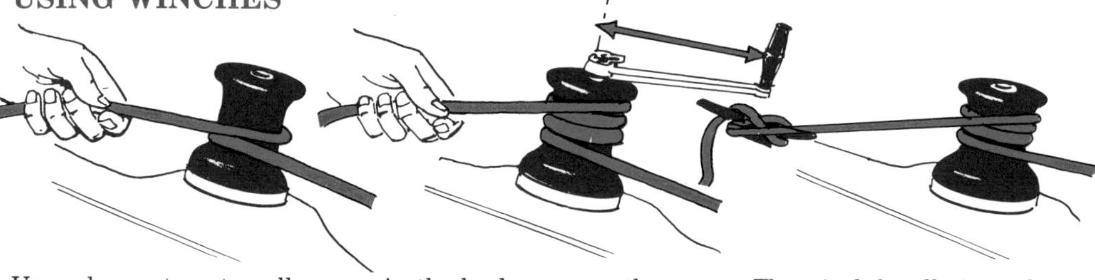

Use only one turn to pull in the slack jib sheet, because if you use more it will probably jam.

As the load comes on the sheet add more turns to increase friction. But, keep pulling on the tail.

The winch handle is used to increase leverage. Wind in the sheet the required amount and secure to cleat.

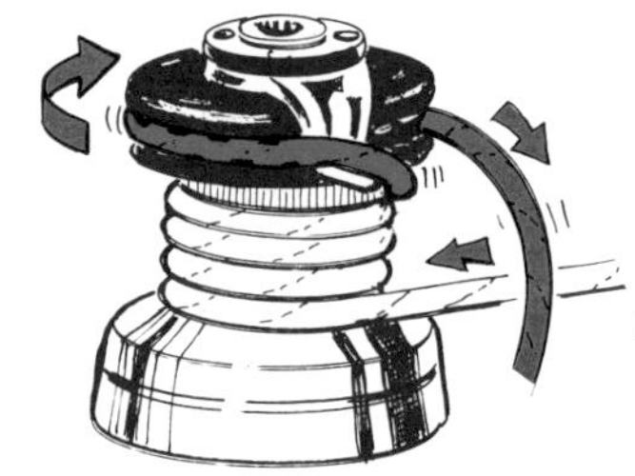

RELEASING

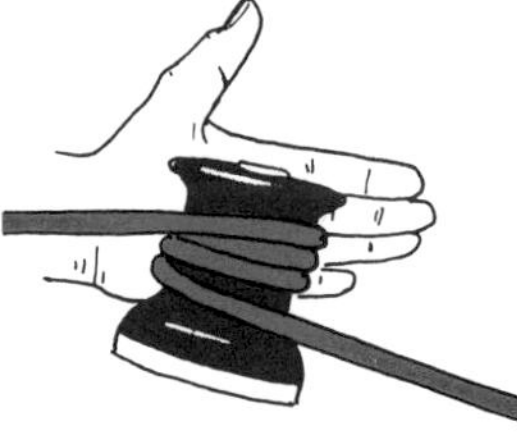

SELF-TAILING WINCH

Here the tail is gripped by the top of the winch so both hands can be used on the handle.

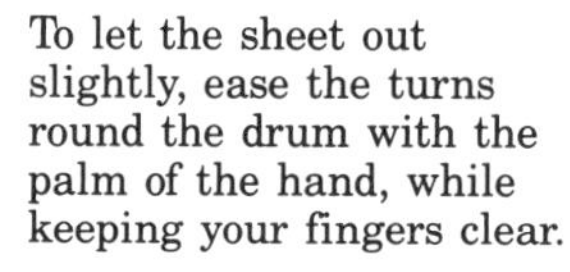

To let the sheet out slightly, ease the turns round the drum with the palm of the hand, while keeping your fingers clear.

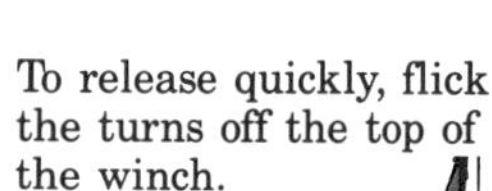

To release quickly, flick the turns off the top of the winch.

For speed, one person can *tail* (**A**) (pull the end of the sheet) while the other *winds* (**B**), putting his whole weight behind the handle. Pulling a loaded line at right angles and quickly taking up the slack is called *swigging* or *sweating* (**C**).

TACKING or going about is putting the bow through the wind.

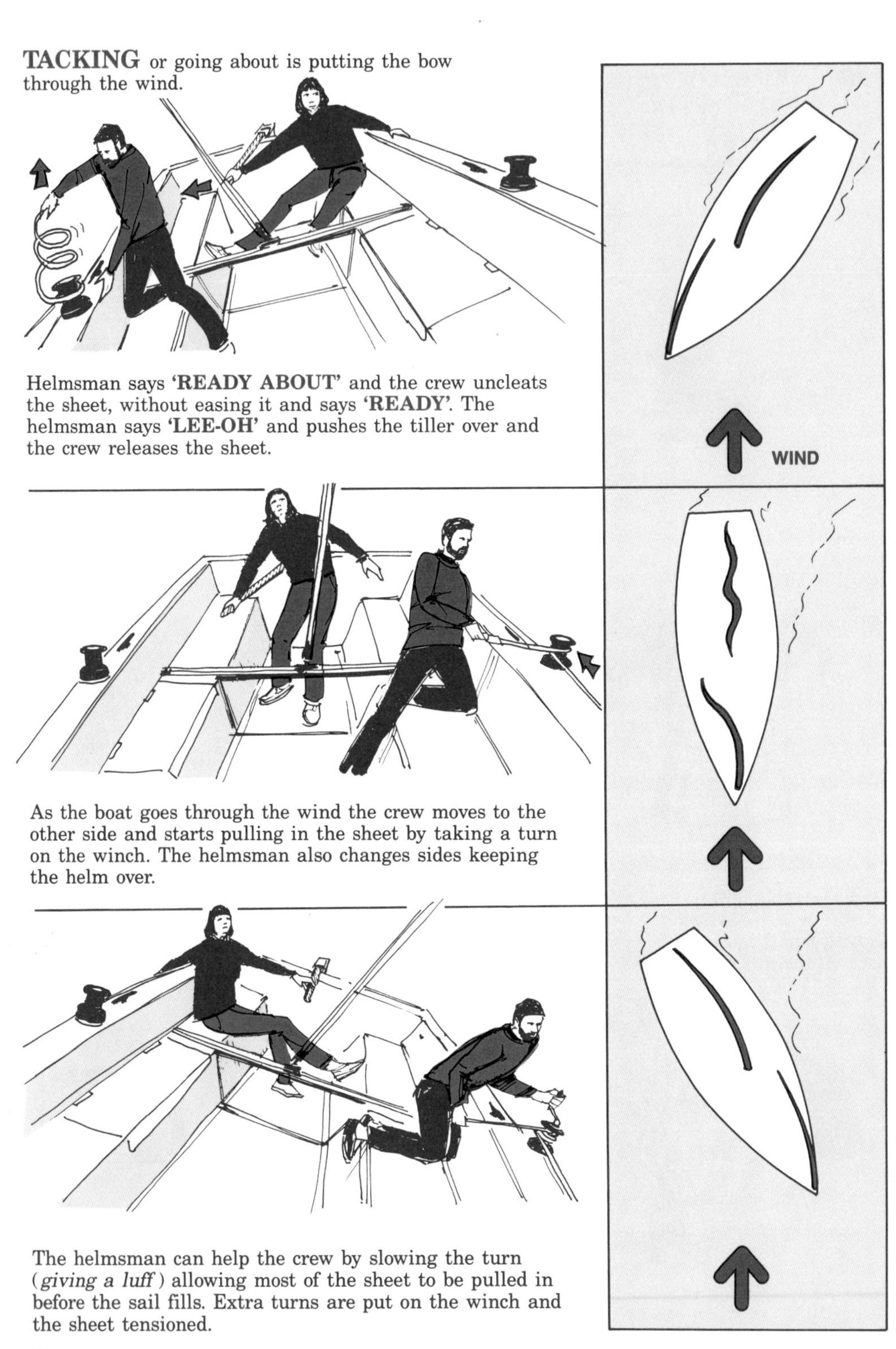

Helmsman says **'READY ABOUT'** and the crew uncleats the sheet, without easing it and says **'READY'**. The helmsman says **'LEE-OH'** and pushes the tiller over and the crew releases the sheet.

As the boat goes through the wind the crew moves to the other side and starts pulling in the sheet by taking a turn on the winch. The helmsman also changes sides keeping the helm over.

The helmsman can help the crew by slowing the turn (*giving a luff*) allowing most of the sheet to be pulled in before the sail fills. Extra turns are put on the winch and the sheet tensioned.

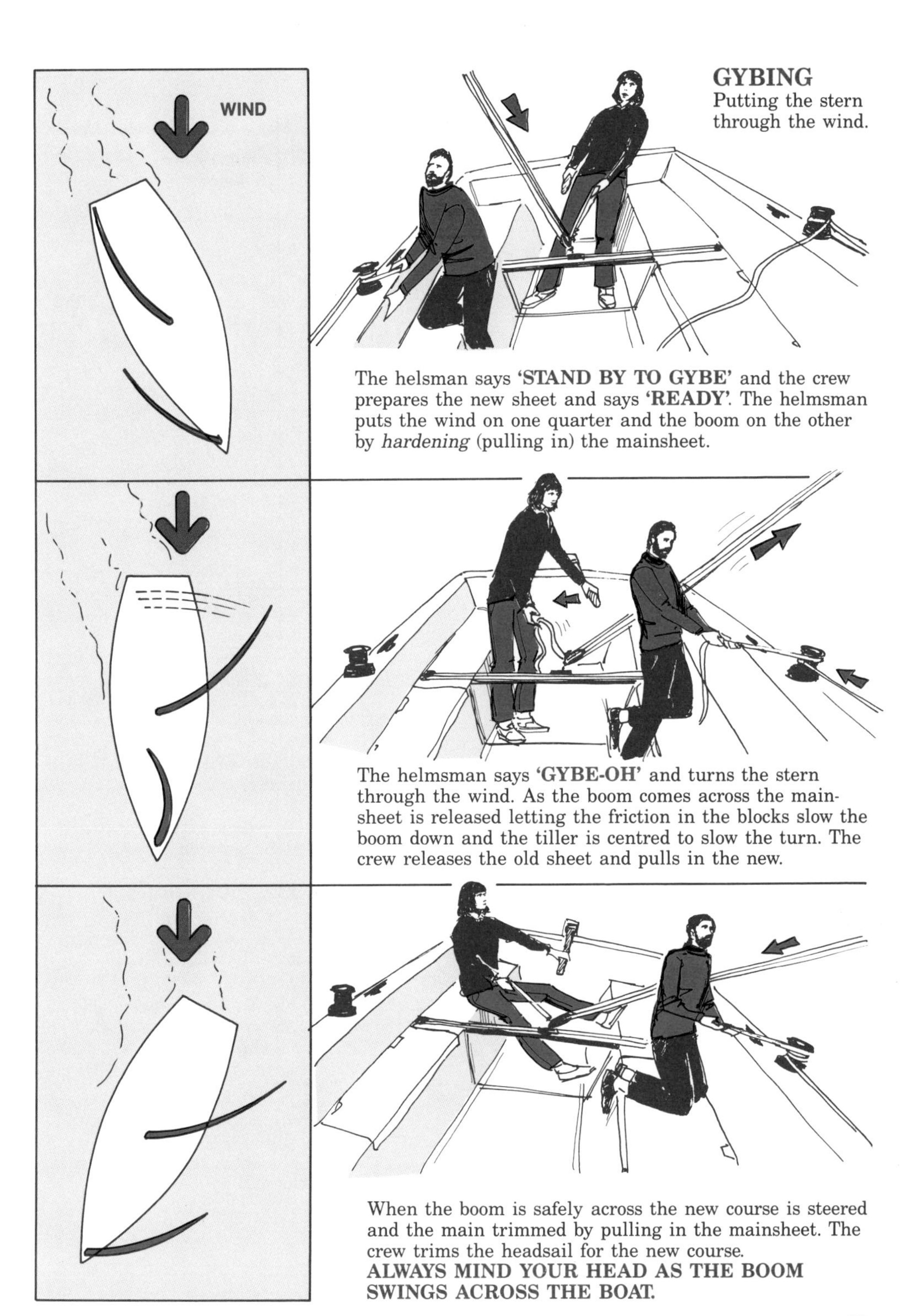

GYBING

Putting the stern through the wind.

The helsman says **'STAND BY TO GYBE'** and the crew prepares the new sheet and says **'READY'**. The helmsman puts the wind on one quarter and the boom on the other by *hardening* (pulling in) the mainsheet.

The helmsman says **'GYBE-OH'** and turns the stern through the wind. As the boom comes across the mainsheet is released letting the friction in the blocks slow the boom down and the tiller is centred to slow the turn. The crew releases the old sheet and pulls in the new.

When the boom is safely across the new course is steered and the main trimmed by pulling in the mainsheet. The crew trims the headsail for the new course.

ALWAYS MIND YOUR HEAD AS THE BOOM SWINGS ACROSS THE BOAT.

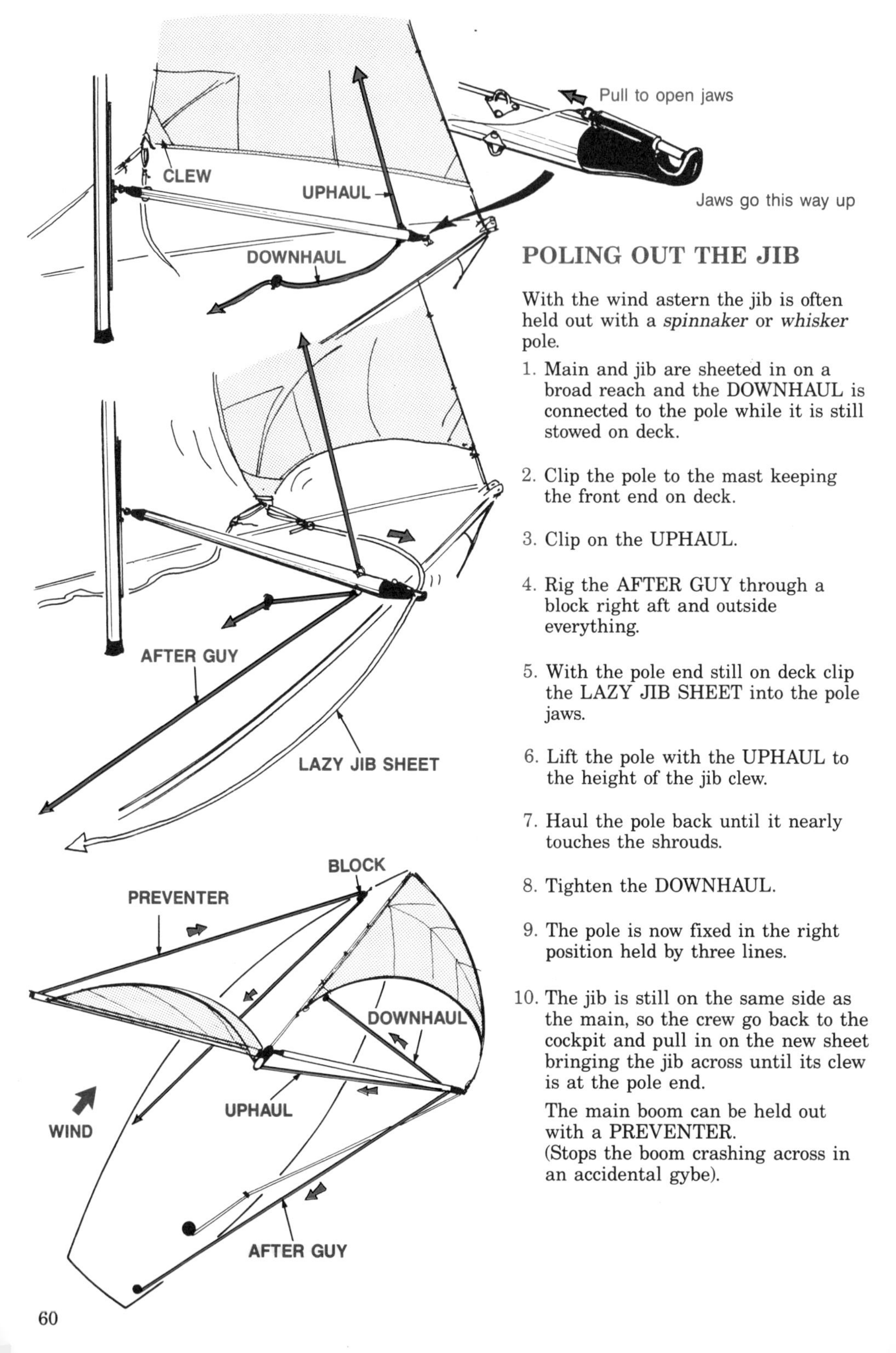

POLING OUT THE JIB

With the wind astern the jib is often held out with a *spinnaker* or *whisker* pole.

1. Main and jib are sheeted in on a broad reach and the DOWNHAUL is connected to the pole while it is still stowed on deck.
2. Clip the pole to the mast keeping the front end on deck.
3. Clip on the UPHAUL.
4. Rig the AFTER GUY through a block right aft and outside everything.
5. With the pole end still on deck clip the LAZY JIB SHEET into the pole jaws.
6. Lift the pole with the UPHAUL to the height of the jib clew.
7. Haul the pole back until it nearly touches the shrouds.
8. Tighten the DOWNHAUL.
9. The pole is now fixed in the right position held by three lines.
10. The jib is still on the same side as the main, so the crew go back to the cockpit and pull in on the new sheet bringing the jib across until its clew is at the pole end.

    The main boom can be held out with a PREVENTER.
    (Stops the boom crashing across in an accidental gybe).

STEERING

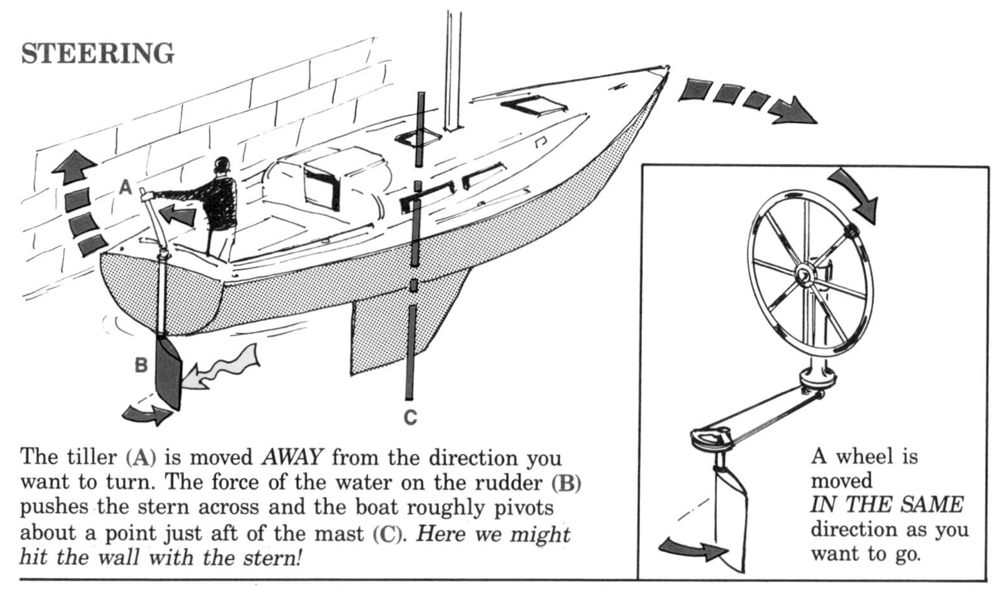

The tiller (A) is moved *AWAY* from the direction you want to turn. The force of the water on the rudder (B) pushes the stern across and the boat roughly pivots about a point just aft of the mast (C). *Here we might hit the wall with the stern!*

A wheel is moved *IN THE SAME* direction as you want to go.

COMPASS COURSE When there are no landmarks the boat is steered by compass.

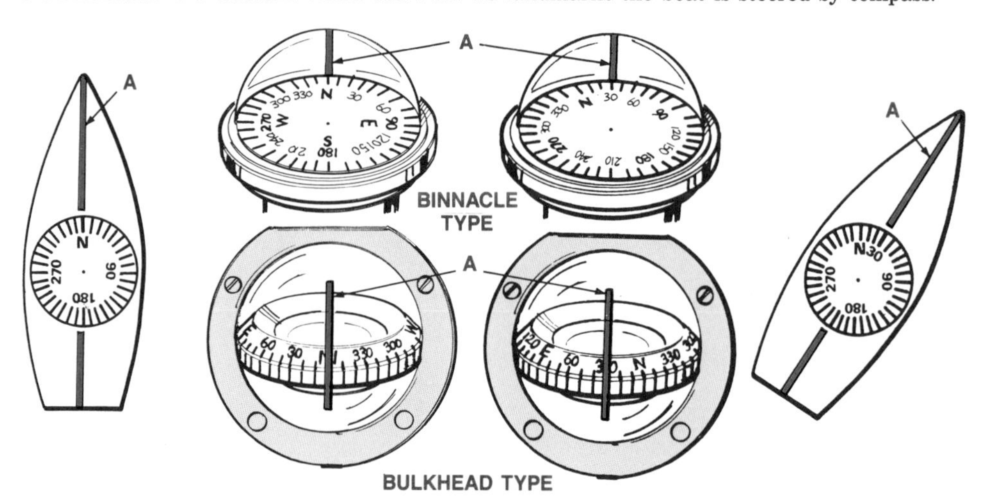

The compass always *STANDS STILL* pointing North while the boat swings around it. The *LUBBER LINE* (A) represents the centre line of the boat. Compasses are usually read from the top as with the BINNACLE TYPE (*note the card markings and the position of the Lubber Line*) or from behind like the BULKHEAD TYPE (*note how the card markings are reversed and the Lubber Line is the other side*).
To turn the boat from North to 030° **STEER THE LUBBER LINE** around to the number. With a bulkhead compass *'push the tiller towards the number you want'*. This may seem confusing but is much simpler when you try it.

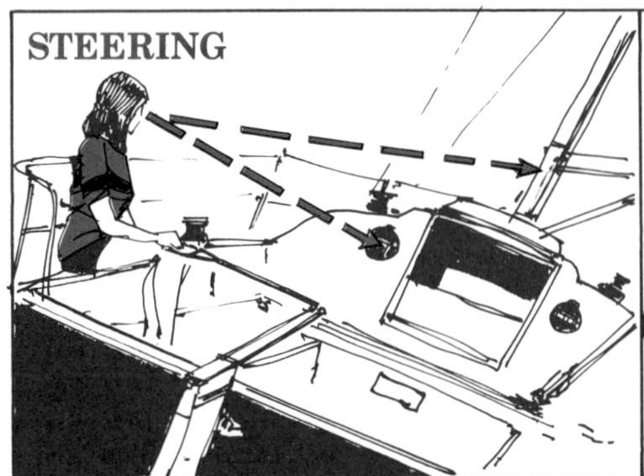

When you're on the correct course, find something ahead that lines up with a piece of the boat. This saves always staring at the compass.

But, don't get transfixed by your steering mark and ignore what is going on around you. ALWAYS keep a good lookout all around especially *behind* you.

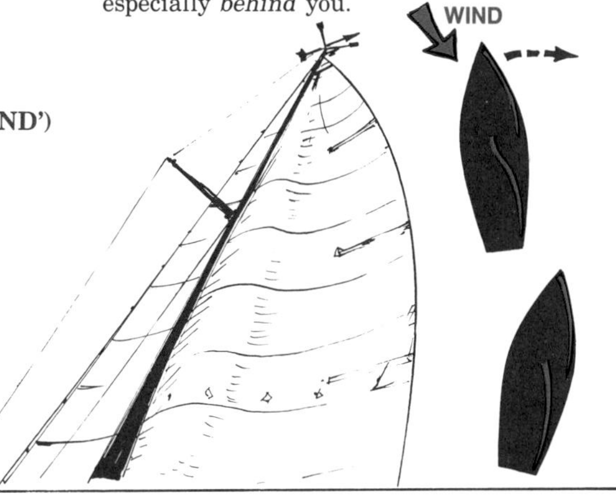

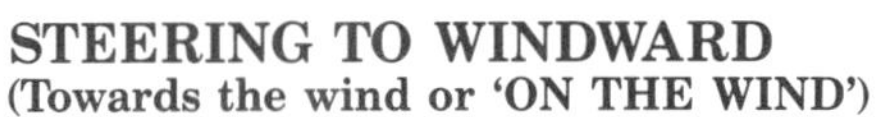

STEERING TO WINDWARD
(Towards the wind or 'ON THE WIND')

With the sails trimmed correctly the helmsman must guard against the wind getting on *the other side of the sail.*

The first indication of this is the front of the mainsail or jib starts to *belly* or *back* so steer the bow *away* from the wind.

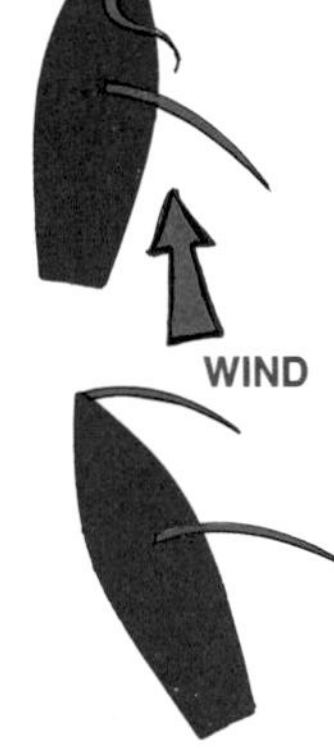

STEERING OFF THE WIND
(Away from the wind)

Here the helmsman must not let the wind get on *the other side of the sail* or it will gybe violently as above.
The first indication of this is the back of the jib *lifting*. Steer the bow *towards* the wind.

(With a tiller push it towards the boom).

IS HE GOING TO HIT US?

Always warn the skipper of any approaching boats. Don't assume they've seen you or know the rule of the road.
(You know how some people drive on the road!)

Does the background move from behind him?

MAINTAINING
A STEADY
COURSE

If vessel maintains the same bearing to you, there will be a collision. Check with a compass or line him up with a stanchion. Also see if the background is moving.

Always keep a good look out all around — especially astern and behind the genoa. Modern ships travel at high speeds, so this can ...

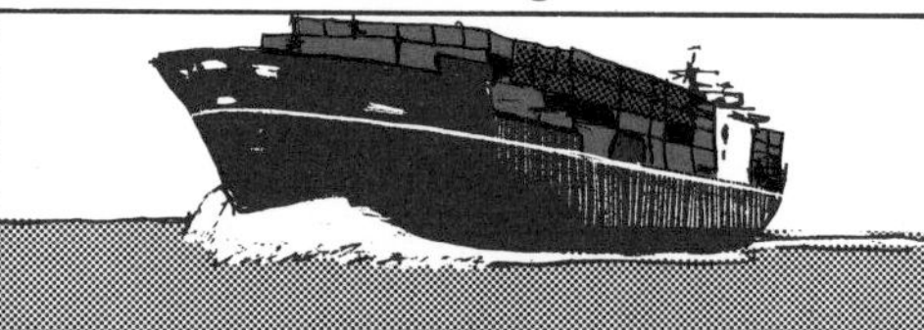

... turn into a huge container ship travelling at over 30 knots and could be on top of you in less than 10 minutes.

At night it's hard to judge distance and easy to convince yourself this is only a small fishing fleet with their deck lights on...

... but, one could be a very fast moving cruise ship ablaze with lights that could be on top of you in a matter of minutes.

In poor visibility, it is often very hard to tell which way a ship is going and it is even harder for him to see you. So, keep the skipper informed of any nearby shipping.

At night the relationship between the ship's two white masthead lights, together with its port and starboard lights show in which direction it is travelling.

Various combinations of coloured lights mean different things — even that he can't manoeuvre to get out of your way ...

... and near the shore these lights can get lost in the background SO KEEP AN EVEN BETTER LOOK OUT AT NIGHT.

WEATHER FORECASTS

These are available on local radio, television, VHF radio or by telephoning a special number. National newspapers publish weather maps and a NAVTEX teleprinter service can also be fitted to your boat. The most common source of weather information is the BBC shipping forecasts which are broadcast at set times each day on the radio.

BEAUFORT SCALE WIND FORCE

Force	Description	Wind speed in knots
1	Light airs, ripples **Drifting conditions**	1-3
2	Light breeze, small wavelets **Both need large sails to catch breeze**	4-6
3	Gentle breeze, crests begin to break **Large headsails & full mainsails**	7-10
4	Moderate, small waves becoming larger, frequent white crests **Reduce headsails and full main (B) might start to reef**	11-16
5	Fresh breeze, moderate waves many white crests, spray **Reduce headsails and (B) starts to reef**	17-21
6	Strong breeze, large waves, white foam crests **Less sail**	22-27
7	Near gale, sea heaps up, white foam, breaking waves blown in streaks **Both under reefed mains with small jibs**	28-33
8	Gale, moderately high waves, breaking crests, foam streaks **Deep reefed mains, storm jib on (B)**	34-40
9	Severe gale, high waves, crests tumble spray affects visibility **(A) Storm jib & trysail, storm jib only on (B)**	41-47
10	STORM Very high waves with long breaking crests. **Survival conditions.**	48-55

REMEMBER – This scale was devised for large sailing vessels and each figure only refers to an AVERAGE speed. So gusts well up into the next force can be expected at times.